Inclusion Works!

Creating Child Care Programs
That Promote Belonging
for Children
with Special Needs

Publishing Information

Inclusion Works! Creating Child Care Programs That Promote Belonging for Children with Special Needs was developed by the Children Development Division, California Department of Education. It was edited by Faye Ong, working in cooperation with Tom Cole, Consultant, Quality Improvement Office. It was prepared for printing by the staff of CDE Press: the cover and interior design were created and prepared by Cheryl McDonald; typesetting was done by Jeannette Reyes. It was published by the Department, 1430 N Street, Sacramento, CA 95814-5901. It was distributed under the provisions of the Library Distribution Act and *Government Code* Section 11096.

ISBN 978-0-8011-1689-6

Ordering Information

Copies of this publication are available for sale from the California Department of Education. For prices and ordering information, please visit the Department Web site at http://www.cde.ca.gov/re/pn or call the CDE Press Sales Office at (800) 995-4099. An illustrated *Educational Resources Catalog* describing publications, videos, and other instructional media available from the Department can be obtained without charge by writing to the CDE Press Sales Office, California Department of Education, 1430 N Street, Suite 3207, Sacramento, CA 95814-5901; FAX (916) 323-0823 or by calling the CDE Press Sales Office at the telephone number shown above.

Notice

The guidance in *Inclusion Works! Creating Child Care Programs That Promote Belonging for Children with Special Needs* is not binding on local educational agencies or other entities. Except for the statutes, regulations, and court decisions that are referenced herein, the document is exemplary, and compliance with it is not mandatory. (See *Education Code* Section 33308.5.)

Contents

A Message from the State Superintendent of Public Instruction

I am pleased to present *Inclusion Works: Creating Child Care Programs That Promote Belonging for Children with Special Needs*, a publication I believe will contribute to the effort to bring the benefits of high-quality care and education to all of California's children, including those with disabilities or other special needs.

Many families rely on child care from the time their children are infants and well into the school years. Child care can be a rich experience in which children and their families gain a sense of belonging to a supportive community. Research shows that all children can benefit from participating in high-quality child care programs that work closely with family members and provide their children with environments, materials, and relationships that enrich learning and development. It is important that we provide the kind of learning environments and care necessary for all children to be successful in the early years as well as in school and later in life.

Approximately 10 percent of children between three and thirteen years of age receive special education services in school. It is critical that children with disabilities or other special needs, and their families, are included in quality child care programs that are the natural environments of their peers who are typically developing. Children learn from their interactions with other children and their surroundings while developing a sense of security and self-esteem from caring relationships with program providers and staff.

Everyone benefits from quality child care programs that provide inclusive care. Children who have a disability or special need get to know and interact with typically developing peers, while their families benefit from programs and services they need to achieve their goals. Children who are typically developing benefit when they have the opportunity to get to know their peers in the classroom. And everyone learns to know one another as human beings with strengths and challenges.

The purpose of this publication is to provide guidance and proven strategies that promote belonging and inclusion for all children. Building on research and the experience of years of effective implementation, this handbook contains stories and examples, as well as background information and resources that support strategies for successful inclusion. By providing the benefit of high-quality child care and education to all of California's children, we will contribute to closing the achievement gap between students with disabilities and students without disabilities.

I hope that the stories and strategies in this document inspire you to open your hearts and programs to all children to support their optimal growth and development.

Jack O'Connell
State Superintendent of Public Instruction

Acknowledgments

The creation of this publication involved individuals from WestEd, the California Childcare Health Program, the California Department of Education, and other representatives from the field who contributed their expertise and time to the writing of this manual:*

Linda Brault, Principal Writer, WestEd Center for Child and Family Studies
Abby J. Cohen, National Child Care Information Center
Lyn Dailey, California Childcare Health Program
Robert Frank, California Childcare Health Program
Eva Guralnick, California Childcare Health Program
Judith Kunitz, California Childcare Health Program
Melissa Ryan, California Childcare Health Program
Pamm Shaw, CEITAN/WestEd
Marsha Sherman, California Childcare Health Program
Rebeca Valdivia, WestEd Center for Child and Family Studies

California Department of Education

Ellen Broms, Consultant, Special Education Division
Meredith Cathcart, Consultant, Special Education Division
Tom Cole, Consultant, Child Development Division
Cecelia Fisher-Dahms, Administrator, Quality Improvement Office, Child Development Division
Mary Hudler, Director, Special Education Division
Greg Hudson, Administrator, Southern Field Services, Child Development Division
Michael Jett, Former Director, Child Development Division
Camille Maben, Director, Child Development Division
Mary Smithberger, Consultant, Child Development Division
Gwen Stephens, Former Assistant Director, Child Development Division
Michael Zito, Head Start Collaboration Office, Child Development Division

Other Contributors

Chris Cleary, Child Care Law Center
Jan Kearns, Shasta County Office of Education
Paul Miller, Tri-Cities Child Care Centers
Susan Sandall, Early Childhood Research Institute on Inclusion (ECRII)

Photographers

Jenn Bartell	Jan Paluck
Jennifer Cheek Pantaléon	Joe Sanberg
Julie Espinoza	Sheila Signer
Mark Lang	Sara Webb-Schmitz

---

*Affiliations were accurate at the time of the development of the document.

Introduction

The purpose of this handbook is to help child care providers learn strategies that promote inclusion of and a sense of belonging for all children. Child care providers who are not accustomed to enrolling children with disabilities or other special needs into their programs will be reassured by the following considerations:

- Child care providers can successfully include children with disabilities or other special needs in the program while promoting belonging for all children.
- Major modifications to their program or facility probably will not be needed in order to include children with disabilities or other special needs.
- Assistance and support for more significant changes in their program or facility may be available.
- An inclusive child care program is rewarding for all the children, families, and staff in child care programs.

Child care offers a rich environment where children learn from their interactions with other children and from their surroundings and where they benefit from caring relationships with program providers and staff. All children, including children with disabilities or other special needs, deserve access to quality child care programs. The information in this handbook is designed to support efforts at making child care programs accessible and inclusive. Most of the suggested accommodations can easily be made with little or no cost. The handbook includes proven strategies, stories of children with special needs who are successfully included in child care programs, and information on making inclusive programs possible.

The biggest barrier to including a child with a disability or other special need seems to be fear—fear not *of* children with special needs but *for* the children. Providers are afraid of physically hurting a child, of not meeting perceived needs, and of having to tell a parent "I do not know how to care for your child." With knowledge, however, this fear fades and competence blooms. *Inclusion Works!* offers a foundation for developing that knowledge and is designed to encourage all child care providers to open their doors—and their hearts—to children with disabilities or other special needs.

The terms and phrases listed below are used differently by different people. What follows are the definitions used in this book. The Glossary at the back may be helpful.

Child care program. Any setting where children are cared for by paid personnel for less than 24 hours a day. This includes child care and development centers, family child care homes, in-home child care, after-school programs, Head Start centers, and the like.

Child care provider. The personnel working in the variety of child care settings who may also be referred to as provider, teacher, caregiver, or staff.

Children with disabilities or other special needs. Includes children with a specific diagnosis, as well as children who do not have a diagnosis but whose behavior, development, and/or health affect their family's ability to maintain child care services. The disability or special need may be as mild as a slight speech delay or as complex as a mixed diagnosis of motor challenges, vision impairment, and cognitive delays. Generally, this definition includes those children who are between birth and twenty-two years of age who are protected by the Americans with Disabilities Act (see Appendix A, "Applicable Laws").

Children who are typically developing. Children who are displaying development and behavior in the expected range for their age.

Inclusion. The full and active participation of children with disabilities or other special needs in community activities, services, and programs designed for typically developing children, including child care. If support, accommodations, or modifications are needed to ensure the child's full, active participation, they are provided appropriately. The participation results in an authentic sense of belonging for the child and family.

Family member or parent. The person with primary responsibility for raising the child. Examples include mothers, fathers, foster parents, and grandparents.

Specialist. Anyone providing intervention, therapy, or treatment services to a child with special needs and his or her family. Examples include special education teacher, speech and language therapist, nurse consultant, social worker, and physical therapist.

1

Including Children with Disabilities or Other Special Needs:

There are many reasons to include children with disabilities or other special needs in child care. Children and families want to be accepted and included in their community regardless of ability. They want to truly belong. But the kind of belonging they desire goes beyond simply "being together." They want full, unconditional membership in family and community. As Norman Kunc, a disability rights advocate, has said so eloquently, "When inclusive education is fully embraced, we abandon the idea that children have to become 'normal' in order to contribute to the world. Instead, we search for and nourish the gifts that are inherent in all people. We begin to look beyond typical ways of becoming valued members of the community and, in doing so, begin to realize the achievable goal of providing all children with an authentic sense of belonging."[1]

Families of children with disabilities or other special need have the same need for child care as do other families. However, families of children with disabilities or special needs often find the search for quality and affordable child care a greater challenge as they face the reluctance of many child care providers to enroll their children. This situation makes it all the more important that child care providers strive to include all children in their programs so as not to increase the immense challenges that such families already face.

Children with disabilities or other special needs may present unique challenges, but the care they need is very similar to that needed by any child. Children with special needs spend most of their time doing what other children do. They have the same curiosity, desire to play, and need to communicate as their peers do. Child care providers who are providing individualized and developmentally appropriate child care already have many of the skills needed to serve children with disabilities or other special needs.

Quality child care contributes to the emotional, social, and intellectual development of children and can also be an important part of school readiness and school success. Children with disabilities or other special needs benefit from quality child care just as much as typically developing children do.

Children with disabilities or other special needs benefit from being in inclusive environments with typically developing children. Studies have shown that inclusive environments, with appropriate help and assistance, allow children to achieve more than they do in segregated environments. When children with disabilities or special needs have all of the opportunities that children who are developing typically have—and especially when they are in an environment with children who are typically developing—they strive toward new goals and achievements, often attaining levels of ability that surprise the adults who care for and about them.

Children who are typically developing benefit from interactions with children who have disabilities or other special needs, as well. Inclusive, supportive environments teach children about differences and about respecting and valuing other people regardless of ability. Children want to help one another as they grow, and when they see adults take steps to support a child, they will take steps to help as well.

Inclusive, supportive environments teach children about differences and about respecting and valuing other people regardless of ability.

Although all children need attention and care, there are children who will require a greater level of support and thoughtful planning.

Turning children away from a child care program solely because they have a disability or other special need is a violation of the Americans with Disabilities Act and California's Unruh Civil Rights Act. Unfortunately, families continue to be routinely refused child care simply because their child has a disability even when their child does not need any special accommodations—a loss for the child, the family, and the child care programs that turn them away. All child care providers need to know that turning a child with special needs away from a child care program may expose the program to significant liability.

Identifying Children with Disabilities or Other Special Needs

All children develop at different rates and in different ways. Some children are born with special needs that can affect their growth and development. Other children may not show developmental problems, delays, or differences until later in childhood.[2] Although all children need attention and care, there are children who will require a greater level of support and thoughtful planning:

- Children identified with a specific diagnosis or disability by medical or educational professionals

- Children who may not have a diagnosis but whose behavior, development, or health affect their family's ability to maintain child care services

Finding out if a child is considered to have a disability or other special need can be a complicated task. Different agencies often use varying criteria for identifying conditions and for determining whether the child and family are eligible for services. (More information on eligibility can be found in Appendix A, "Applicable Laws.") Generally, in order for a child to be eligible for early intervention or special education services, he or she must show a delay in one or more areas of development. In addition, children identified through the early intervention system may be "at risk" of a developmental delay. Public schools and the early intervention system are the most common agencies for providing support and services to children with disabilities or special needs in child care settings.

To be eligible for special education services, children must meet certain criteria in one or more categories of disabilities. These categories are broader than labels such as Down syndrome, cerebral palsy, and so forth. Children with the same diagnosis may be placed into several different categories, depending on other factors.

Most children from birth through age fourteen (over 70 percent) identified by special education professionals as having a disability have delays in learning and communication (see Appendix D, "California Children Enrolled in Special Education"). What is more important is that learning disabilities are often not recognized or identified until children begin formal schooling. Children who learn differently or have delays in language commonly manifest special needs through their behavior in group settings. Child care providers can provide a language-rich environment and make accommodations based on knowledge of the individual child.

There are fewer children with more significant disabilities such as mental retardation, physical and mobility impairments, or multiple disabilities. When children do have significant disabilities, they are likely to be receiving specialized services that may support success in a child care setting. Children who are eligible for and who receive early intervention or special education services have individual plans with goals and strategies for caregivers and providers to use. For children under age three, the plans are called individualized family services plans (IFSPs); for children over age three, the plans are called individualized education programs (IEPs). Child care providers can be an important member of an IFSP or IEP team when these plans are being developed. More information about IEPs and IFSPs is available in the Glossary.

When serving an individual child, however, the provider should focus on the child's needs, not the disability or its label.

Learning about Individual Children

Information about a specific disability may give a child care provider ideas for how to support a child (see Appendix B, "Resources"). When serving an individual child, however, the provider should focus on the child's needs, not the disability or its label. A child with cerebral palsy, for example, may walk with leg braces, use a wheelchair, have minor physical symptoms, or demonstrate a delay in using language. The possible variations within this one label are tremendous, demonstrating that no single label or diagnosis can provide enough information about a particular child. Child care providers need to learn beyond a textbook definition and ask questions with sensitivity and understanding—particularly in talks with parents. Providers can go far toward setting a tone of welcome and understanding. When a family member shares a child's diagnosis, a good follow-up question is often "And how does that affect _____'s development?"

For example, if a parent calls and says "I'm looking for a preschool for my child. She has Down syndrome. Is your school good for her?" The following response would be appropriate: "Our school has many wonderful things to offer. It may be a great place for you and your daughter. I would love to hear more about her interests and strengths. I'm sure that you have many questions that I can answer for you. In order to help me address these questions, may I ask how her Down syndrome affects her development?" This approach can help assure a family member that the child care provider is sincerely concerned about the success of the child and is interested in providing appropriate, individually tailored care.

The response from the parent will help the child care provider determine what accommodations might be needed, what other questions may be appropriate to ask, and whether specialists are involved or needed. (Chapter 4 presents information on working collaboratively with specialists.)

2

Comparing Inclusive Child Care and Quality Child Care Settings

Quality child care is evident when each child grows and learns, families feel confident and secure, and providers are qualified and stable.

M any child care providers are surprised to learn that there is very little difference between inclusive child care and general, quality child care. Quality child care is evident when each child grows and learns, families feel confident and secure, and providers are qualified and stable. Current research provides a number of descriptions:

> Quality child care enables a young child to become emotionally secure, socially competent, and intellectually capable. The single most important factor in quality care is the relationship between the child and the caregiver. Children who receive warm and sensitive caregiving are more likely to trust caregivers, to enter school ready and eager to learn, and to get along well with other children. The quality of caregiver-child relations depends in part on the sensitivity of the caregiver and in part on the ratio of caregivers to children, the number of children in a group, and the education and training levels of the caregiver. A quality program also attends to the basic issues of health and safety and emphasizes a partnership between parents and caregivers.
>
> Starting Points[3]

> . . . Child care situations with safer, cleaner, more stimulating physical environments and smaller group sizes, lower child–adult ratios, and care givers who allowed children to express their feelings and took their views into account also had care givers who were observed to provide more sensitive, responsive, and cognitively stimulating care—quality of care that was expected to be associated with better developmental outcomes for children.
>
> The National Institute of Child Health and Human Development[4]

Child Care Aware, an organization supported by the Child Care Bureau of the U.S. Department of Health and Human Services, has identified five key indicators of quality inclusive child care:[5]

- A positive and healthy learning environment
- The right number and mix of children and adults
- Trained and supported personnel
- A developmental focus on the child
- Parents treated as partners

These indicators are clearly part of all quality child care programs. The developmentally appropriate practices identified by the National Association for the Education of Young Children (NAEYC) provide additional indicators of quality. NAEYC posits that the use of developmentally appropriate practices results in high-quality care for *all* children, including those with disabilities or special needs.

Professionals constantly make decisions that affect the well-being and education of children. When these decisions are based on the following three important kinds of information or knowledge, developmentally appropriate practices are certain to emerge.[6]

- **Age appropriateness** refers to what is known about child development and learning and the activities, materials, interactions, or experiences that will be safe, healthy, interesting, achievable, and challenging to children (depending on, and varying with, the age of the children).
- **Individual appropriateness** relates to what is known about the strengths, interests, and needs of each individual child in the group.
- **Cultural/social influences** are what a child care provider knows about the cultural and social contexts in which children live. Paying attention to these influences ensures that learning experiences are designed to be meaningful, *relevant,* and respectful of the participating children and their families.

Infants and toddlers in group care benefit from "an educator who is loving and responsive, respects the baby's individuality, and offers good surroundings."[7]

Since most definitions of quality care include meeting the needs of the individual child, quality child care is good for *all* children. And, not surprisingly, high-quality settings have more success fostering a sense of belonging, physical development, and intellectual abilities in children with disabilities or special needs.

Promoting Inclusive Practices

Brochures, parent handbooks, and other written material regularly used in a child care setting can set the tone of inclusion and belonging. If a program's existing documents already include phrases that emphasize welcoming *all* children or embracing diversity, it is relatively easy to add statements that include diversity of ability, as well. The inclusive, welcoming language in the statements below suggest ways to present the good news of an inclusive program:

- "Our early childhood teachers' strong knowledge of child development helps them to teach all young children whatever their talents, interests, and abilities."

Individual appropriateness relates to what is known about the strengths, interests, and needs of each individual child in the group.

9

- "We take pride in our inclusive program. Our teachers adapt activities to include all students, recognizing that their individual goals may be different. At times, our providers and children may receive assistance from specialists, such as special educators, physical therapists, and other school or early intervention personnel, who recognize the individual interests and strengths of children."

The following examples are taken from an online brochure for an existing center.[8]

- "The National Child Research Center provides a collaborative approach to preschool education in an environment that nurtures the whole child, fosters partnerships with families, and is committed to the inclusion of children with special needs."
- "A highly trained, multidisciplinary faculty employs developmentally appropriate practices, supported by ongoing professional development and sound research. Essential to its role as a model of early childhood education is the creation of a diverse, respectful community. Both within and beyond the school community, NCRC seeks opportunities to advocate for all children and their families."

Even if children with disabilities are not currently enrolled in a child care setting, providers can still promote inclusive practices. One way is to have pictures, books, and materials that present children with disabilities in a general setting. How people are alike and different naturally arises in a child care setting; a caregiver can take advantage of these opportunities to discuss them. Language use is also critical in developing an atmosphere of inclusion. The best practice is to use "person-first" language when one is talking about people with disabilities. This practice simply means putting the person before the disability: "a child with autism" rather than "an autistic child."

The process of exploring inclusion with families, colleagues, and children will suggest other ways to expand inclusive practices. For example, planning staff discussions on specific changes in philosophy, attitudes, and practices goes far toward including children with special needs in a child care setting. Outside the immediate child care setting, adults with disabilities in a community might contribute to a care provider's expanding knowledge of issues related specifically to inclusion and to disabilities in general. Additional resources are available in Appendix B, "Resources."

How people are alike and different naturally arises in a child care setting; a caregiver can take advantage of these opportunities to discuss them.

3

Creating Inclusive Child Care Settings

Programs that are committed to quality and diversity often see belonging and inclusion as the starting point for all children.

Programs that are committed to quality and diversity often see belonging and inclusion as the starting point for all children. The Americans with Disabilities Act and California's Unruh Civil Rights Act (see Appendix A, "Applicable Laws") make it illegal for a child care provider to refuse to serve a child solely on the basis of a disability. There is, however, a significant difference between providers who enroll children with disabilities or other special needs because it is the law and providers who reach out and welcome all children into their care.

Factors for Success

A great deal of research has been conducted on what makes inclusion of all children work. The Early Childhood Research Institute on Inclusion (ECRII), a national research project funded by the U.S. Department of Education, identified the following six factors as the key to initiating and implementing inclusive practices:[9]

1. Providers or staff members are passionate about making inclusion work. This factor was the strongest and could include providers, teachers, program administrators, and even a district's director of special education.

2. A vision of inclusive practice developed over time by respecting and considering the views of everyone involved in implementation is shared by all.

3. State and national policies "prompt" programs to become inclusive. One example is the 1972 policy that required that 10 percent of a Head Start program's enrollment be made up of children with disabilities. Some effective programs are also found in states that have state-level policies about inclusion, as well.

4. Additional money, training by qualified consultants, or other type of support is provided for inclusive child care programs.

5. At the program or district level, support is given to enhance collaboration and communication among people involved in providing inclusive programs.

6. A passionate community of individuals, such as parents or other community advocates, works to spark interest in implementing inclusive programs.

Daily Success

As each child is unique, so is each child care program. There is no magic formula for making inclusion work beyond the creativity, energy, and interest that most child care providers already bring to their work. Their uniqueness notwithstanding, every program is able to successfully include children with disabilities. And each makes it work child by child, day by day. A "can-do" attitude among the providers helps to provide the necessary energy for coming up with solutions to the inevitable challenges. It also helps to have an enthusiastic attitude on how to make inclusion work rather than to simply fulfill a legal obligation.

Some children need small changes to the curriculum or minor supports in order to get the most out of certain activities. These sorts of things may consist of fairly simple accommodations, such as providing a special place or quiet activity for a child who is unable to participate in large-group activities or making available a special snack for a child who needs to eat more frequently than the typical meal or snack schedule.

Other children may require more specific adaptations that might not be readily apparent. A variety of community resources can be helpful in determining what those might be. The family, for example, is always the first and most important guide for what a child might need; after that, an area specialist or a local workshop might be. Beyond the immediate community, a world of literature in books, periodicals, and Web sites devoted to disabilities and inclusion can inform a child care provider about appropriate adaptations for a child with a particular condition or need. Refer to Appendix B, "Resources."

Programs that begin with a high-quality, developmentally appropriate foundation; a positive attitude on the part of the care provider; appropriate adult–child ratios; supportive administrators; and adequate

There is no magic formula for making inclusion work beyond the creativity, energy, and interest that most child care providers already bring to their work.

One of the biggest roles for a care provider is to facilitate a sense of belonging and inclusion.

training for the provider will be in a good position to creatively solve problems for a child with disabilities or other special needs, exactly as it does for children who are typically developing. If a child already has an established diagnosis, trained intervention personnel may be available to assist in this process. One of the biggest roles for a care provider is to facilitate a sense of belonging and inclusion. Several helpful strategies are as follows:[10]

- Start with the assumption that all children are competent.
- Adapt the environment so that it is developmentally appropriate, challenging, and fits the needs and interests of each child.
- While there may be a need to support a child's mastery of a specific skill, keep the whole child in mind, particularly the child's social-emotional experience.

Consider the following questions when adapting an activity for a child with special needs:

- Does the child have an opportunity to be in control of the learning experience?
- Is there a balance between adult-initiated learning and child-initiated learning?
- Can the child make choices while learning the skill?
- Is the child able to initiate his/her own efforts to practice the skill, with support given by the child care provider?
- Is the child gaining self-confidence and showing the joy of accomplishment while learning?
- Is there room in the activity for the child to make discoveries?

Common Modifications, Adaptations, and Supports

Each child is an individual, and modifications, adaptations, accommodations, and supports should be designed with a single child in mind. However, researchers from the Early Childhood Research Institute on Inclusion (ECRII) have found that many changes can be grouped into categories of modifications. Several of these categories are used in various child care programs that include children with disabilities or special needs.[11] The most common categories and brief descriptions are included below. More detailed illustrations and stories are in chapter 5, "Examples of Inclusive Child Care Strategies."

STRATEGY
1 Environmental Support

Alter the physical, social, or temporal environment to promote participation, engagement, and learning.

Examples:

- Use a photo, picture, or object to signal the next activity.
- Make boundaries for activities (e.g., mark sections of the floor with tape, provide a tray or box lid for art activities).
- Free surfaces of bumps or smooth them with "lips" and ramps.

(See detailed story on page 34)

Alter the physical, social, or temporal environment to promote participation, engagement, and learning.

STRATEGY
2 Materials Adaptation

Modify materials to promote independence.

Examples:

- Add knobs to wooden puzzles.
- Use fabric self-adhesive closures on dress-up clothes.
- Place "no-slip" placemats under dishes when children eat or serve themselves.

(See detailed story on page 38)

STRATEGY

Activity Simplification

Simplify a complicated task by breaking it into smaller parts or reducing the number of steps.

Examples:

- Give a child materials for a task one piece at a time.
- Prepare materials for easier use (e.g., peel the background off stickers and bend them so they lift off easily).
- Replace materials that may be difficult to use with ones that are simpler and can serve the same function (e.g., use a squeeze bottle instead of a pump dispenser).

(See detailed story on page 40)

Replace materials that may be difficult to use with ones that are simpler and can serve the same function

---

 STRATEGY

Child Preferences

Capitalize on a child's favorite activities.

Examples:

- Observe a child's interests and then provide additional materials or toys that match them.
- Use the child's preferred activities, such as music, to support efforts to learn other skills.
- Find ways to build on a child's preferred activities when introducing new ideas.

(See detailed story on page 42)

STRATEGY

5 Special Equipment

Use adaptive devices to facilitate participation.

Examples:

- Ensure that providers know the proper use of adaptive or medical equipment, such as hearing aids, glasses, or nebulizers (following licensing requirements and pediatrician or specialist recommendations) and the need for vigilance by adults when this equipment is present.
- Allow all children to participate in activities by providing appropriate seating or other equipment, such as a plastic chair near the water table for a child who uses a wheelchair.
- Use picture cards or electronic switch-activated speaking devices for children who cannot speak, allowing them to communicate their choices.

(See detailed story on page 44)

STRATEGY

6 Adult Support

Employ direct adult intervention to support a child's efforts.

Examples:

- Assign a primary caregiver to a child so that the assigned adult is able to know the unique needs of the child and ways to support him/her.
- Provide direct instruction or guidance to a child while he/she is learning or practicing tasks.
- Learn specific ways of interacting or communicating with a child, such as sign language.

(See detailed stories on pages 46 and 49)

Provide direct instruction or guidance to a child while he/she is learning or practicing tasks.

STRATEGY

7 Peer Support

Use classmates as models to help children learn.

Examples:

- Pair a child with a certain disability with a child who does not have that disability during certain activities, such as eating, class chores, and so on, ensuring that the child with special needs is sometimes the helper and not always the one being helped.
- Facilitate children's interactions and observations of one another in small groups.
- Teach children specific ways to engage and interact with a child with special needs.

(See detailed story on page 52)

STRATEGY

8 Invisible Support

Arrange naturally occurring events to assist inclusion.

Examples:

- Stock the dress-up center or kitchen corner with sufficient items so more children can participate in a popular activity without competition.
- Assign roles during children's play, such as having a child with limited mobility be in charge of "pumping gas" as the children riding bikes go by.
- Comment on children's play in ways that encourage further interaction.

(See detailed story on page 54)

Identifying and Finding Help

4

Child care providers are often the first to notice a child who is learning, communicating, or developing in a way that is different from other children in their care.

Child care providers are often the first to notice a child who is learning, communicating, or developing in a way that is different from other children in their care; or a child care provider may be the first person whom family members approach with their concerns. When a critical difference is noted after careful observation and intervention with a particular child does not seem to be working, the next step involves looking for additional help to foster the child's sense of belonging. Although this help can come from the family, more expertise is often needed, such as advice or insight from the child's pediatrician or health-care provider, or from the child's therapist or other specialist.

Referral to a Specialist

When a child care provider recommends that a family seek help from a pediatrician or specialists, or if family members grant a child care provider the necessary permission to seek help, the child care provider is "making a referral." A referral requires talking to the parents of the child first. They must give their written permission (consent) before seeking other assistance. Parents sometimes want to pursue assistance themselves.

Talks with Parents

Communicating concerns about a child to the parents is often a difficult step. Success is more likely if this step is taken from an already-existing relationship that is built on trust and respect. Even when this relationship is in place, child care providers still need to plan what they will say about concerns for the child. Any techniques used for effective parent conferences can apply here. A discussion of this nature should take place in a private location, with adequate time allowed, and, if applicable, both parents in attendance.

The first step is to ask the family members how they see the child and then to share the positive qualities observed within the care setting. At the outset, it is helpful for child care providers to let the family know that:

- They share concerns for the child.
- Their intent is to support the child's development.

In order to do this, they need to get some ideas for how to best meet the child's needs. If family members differ in their view of the child, be open to their perspective, ask questions, gather information, and invite them to be your partner in meeting the needs of their child. When done respectfully, this communication can lead to a fruitful exchange of ideas and ultimately help for the child.

Documentation of Concerns

When it is time to share concerns about a child, clear communication becomes vital—communication with concrete examples and without judgment. For instance, rather than insist that a child is "behaving badly and bothering other children," a provider would be more effective by letting the parents know that certain observations have been documented: their child has a harder time sitting still than do other children, does not cope well with transitions, and has had five incidents of hitting other children during the last week.

When it is time to share concerns about a child, clear communication becomes vital— communication with concrete examples and without judgment.

It is especially important that observations be shared without labels or diagnoses (for example, attention deficit disorder). Most child care providers are not qualified to provide such a diagnosis, and doing so often gets in the way of the next step in the referral process. On the other hand, specific observations and descriptions of what is happening will be helpful to any specialists who become involved.

Supporting the Family by Providing Access to Services

Families often need and appreciate support in getting help. Many families report fear that a provider will reject their child or them if their child needs extra help, which may make them reluctant to approach a child care provider with this need. An inclusive child care provider lets the appropriate family members know that everything will be done to support the child and to incorporate any new ideas into the program's procedures, curriculum, and activities. When everything is in place to refer the child to an early intervention program, local school district, or pediatrician/health-care provider, the family needs to be allowed to take the lead. For those families that want to actively explore additional sources of support for their child, a child care provider can then talk with them about where to go and how to obtain further assessment and/or possible services.

This is the point at which the child care provider is "making a referral." In this process, it is generally appropriate to refer the family to their pediatrician and to a local early intervention/special education resource at the same time. Information about these kinds of services is available within most care programs, local early intervention services, special education services, and other resources. By sharing concrete

An inclusive child care provider lets the appropriate family members know that everything will be done to support the child and to incorporate any new ideas into the program's procedures, curriculum, and activities.

observations and pertinent information throughout the process, a child care provider succeeds in helping family members clarify their questions about their child and giving them an idea of what the referral will accomplish.

Calling resource agencies in advance to get information for the parents can be very helpful. However, no one can guarantee eligibility or services from another agency to a family. A better approach for a child care provider is to describe what might happen after the referral and what the possible outcomes might be on the basis of past experience. A child care provider can also offer to be a source of information to the referral source. Confidentiality issues are sacred, so parents must give permission for anyone, including a child care provider, to talk about their child with referral sources. In California, the Child Care Health Line (800-333-3212) is also available to providers and families to facilitate the linkages with special service providers. Most communities also have California Early Start Family Resource Centers (see Appendix B, "Resources") to help parents with linkages and an understanding of their rights to services.

When family members want access to other resources, they need to consider important issues, such as insurance, linguistic fluency, cultural practices, transportation, and any previous uncomfortable or negative experiences with authority figures, such as teachers or doctors. Commonly, a child care provider helps a family obtain the services their child needs by setting the process in motion for them. At the same time, it is important that the child care provider not do too much for the family or feel responsible for resolving every issue. The provider can be more helpful for everyone involved by focusing on supporting the family as it moves through the process. Finding ways to meet the child's needs will best serve the family and the child in the long run.

Confidentiality issues are sacred, so parents must give permission for anyone, including a child care provider, to talk about their child with referral sources.

Supporting a Family That Declines Services

Sometimes family members may choose not to pursue resources when they first hear a child care provider's concerns about their child; or they may be open to information yet not take action immediately. Child care providers must remember that everyone moves at a different pace and accepts information differently. These differences are often greatly influenced by a family's emotional response, which greatly affects what they are able to hear and understand. Processing and integrating this information will take time. The idea that their child may be different from other children is hard for some families to accept. Unless behavioral or other issues, such as medical urgency, makes it impossible to care appropriately for the child without assistance, child care providers must allow a family to proceed on its own timeline. A child care provider's role under these circumstances is to support a family in understanding the information that has been shared, to repeat the information whenever necessary, and to remind them that additional resources and information are available whenever they want it.

If a child care provider's own judgment or emotions interfere with the ability to respect the family as the decision maker, the child care provider should seek personal/professional support and then suggest that the family discuss this with someone else as well. If a child care provider believes that a family's refusal to seek help constitutes negligence, then that provider has an obligation to be clear with the family about the critical nature of the concerns presented. At that point it is time for the child care provider to proceed with a referral, independent of the family's involvement.

In many cases, it is appropriate to have a family talk about concerns with the primary health-care provider. Some issues faced by children with disabilities or other special needs are medical and require careful follow-up by a health-care provider.

Health and Medical Service Systems

Although some health-care providers have little knowledge of the assessment and service issues that are essential to working effectively with children with special needs, others specialize in this area. Parents and providers must be proactive to ensure a good match between child and primary health-care provider.

Often it is a good idea for a referral to be made to the special education/ early intervention service system while the referral to the health-care provider is being made. Because the referral process takes time, referring to only one system (such as health care) may delay admission to the other (such as early intervention). Referrals are best made directly by the family. If a provider makes a referral, the family must have provided clear permission.

Local Special Education/Early Intervention Service Systems

Local special education/early intervention service systems are required by law to engage in child find. This term means that an active and ongoing effort needs to made by the specialist system to identify children who may be eligible for services. Some areas may provide free screenings at local child care settings, while others may send outreach materials to child care and medical agencies. Not all children with differences in their development will qualify for services from special education/early intervention. Appropriate screening and assessment are generally required to make this determination. These procedures are provided to families free of charge, as are most special education services.

After a referral is made, the special education/early intervention agency has 60 calendar days (45 for children under age three) to complete the assessment, determine eligibility, and hold a meeting to plan for services, if needed. Again, referrals are best made directly by the family. If a provider makes a referral, the family must have provided clear permission.

Not all children with differences in their development will qualify for services from special education/early intervention.

If a child care provider suspects that a child in a care setting may have special needs, that individual should encourage the child's parents to call the local school district or the special education program of the county office of education to request an assessment. For concerns regarding children from birth to age three, families may call the California Department of Developmental Services (800-515-BABY[2229]). They will be provided with information on resources in their local community, including the regional center or their California Early Start Family Resource Center for parent-to-parent support.

Once a referral is received, representatives of those agencies will talk with the family and may schedule an assessment to see if the child qualifies for services. Knowing the best person to contact and his or her telephone number in a school district can be of great help to the family. The local California Early Start Family Resource Center (see Appendix B, "Resources") usually has this information. There are several important things for parents to know when they contact these agencies:

- The agencies operate under legal timelines for responding to parents' requests for consideration of early intervention or special education services (parents may want to put their request in writing if they are having difficulty getting a response).
- Parents must give written permission for their child to be tested and receive early intervention or special education.
- All services are confidential and provided at no cost to the family.

Even if a child is not found eligible for special education services, the team providing the assessment may have suggestions for ways to support the child's growth and development.

Even if a child is not found eligible for special education services, the team providing the assessment may have suggestions for ways to support the child's growth and development. Parents might appreciate being made aware of this possibility and be encouraged to take advantage of the information provided. Additionally, the assessment team will be able to give guidelines for monitoring the child's progress as the child becomes older. Guidelines are helpful in case the family or others become concerned over later-developing behaviors or challenges with the child.

If the child referred is found eligible and begins to receive services, the child can benefit from the child care provider working with the specialists who provide the service. The specialists can then become consultants to the child care provider and the family. The next chapter offers ideas for ways to maximize this kind of collaboration.

5

Collaborating
for Inclusion

To effectively meet the needs of children with differing abilities and learning characteristics, child care providers may need to expand the way in which they reach out to families and link with specialists. These two groups of people have important information to share and can serve as resources to support children in a program. Their suggestions invariably enrich efforts at inclusion. Specialists themselves may even be able to visit a care facility and offer some on-site guidance.

Providing inclusive child care does not mean a provider—or even a group of providers—has to do the work alone. Everyone has a role to play. The primary role of a child care provider is to nurture and support the child's development in a loving and caring manner. Partnerships formed with other adults who are caring for the child—the parents, health-care providers, or specialists—can complement the efforts of all concerned, especially when everyone concentrates on a particular strength. When the expertise of many are combined, ideas develop and strategies emerge that are better than those any one person could have developed alone.[12] The result is the essence of true collaboration.

For collaboration to be successful, the following elements are essential:

- **Respect for family members' knowledge and experience with the child.** Family members are a provider's first and best resource; they should be included in the planning and implementation of care for their children.

- **Clear and regular communication.** Planned meetings and informal conversations are arranged with everyone involved in a child's development. These occasions are ideal opportunities to discuss what works and what needs improvement and to practice all-important communication skills—asking questions, listening carefully, and sharing concerns. If what is discussed needs to be reflected in the individualized family service plan/individual education program

The primary role of a child care provider is to nurture and support the child's development in a loving and caring manner.

(IFSP/IEP), the child care provider needs to specifically ask how that will happen.

- **Time reserved for collaboration.** Commonly, nearly everyone involved in supporting a child with a disability or special need will be pressed for time. The commitment to collaboration includes an understanding that reserving the time to plan, interact, communicate, and evaluate will actually save time in the long run.

- **An investment in the inclusive program.** All providers need to be actively involved in developing the inclusive program and feel personally interested in its success. If teachers support inclusive practices, but the program's administrators do not, the most valiant efforts are not likely to be successful.

- **Collaborative efforts with the family and specialists to obtain appropriate assessment and the support services that can be provided in a program.** If a child is eligible for specialized services, a child care provider can and should participate in IFSP or IEP meetings and in the planning and delivery of services if a parent requests the caregiver's participation. Sometimes a specialist will be able to come into the child care program regularly; at other times the specialist will be able to serve as an outside consultant. Additional suggestions for ways to obtain and utilize specialists are included in chapter 4, "Identifying and Finding Help."

Contributing to Collaboration

There are many ways child care providers contribute to collaboration with family members and specialists. One of the gifts a child care provider can bring to collaboration around a particular child is to focus on the child first—not on the disability or challenging areas. Some additional ideas for ways to collaborate are listed below.

- **Gather multiple perspectives.** Child care providers often have a great understanding and perspective on what is important for a child from their knowledge of child development and their observations of other children in the program. The family members have a very different, deeper knowledge of the child, while the specialists offer insight based on their training and experience.

- **Seek assistance as soon as possible.** If there is concern about a child with disabilities or special needs who is included in a child care program, a child care provider would be wise to document concerns and work with the family and specialists to get support. Sometimes problems in inclusion arise from an inappropriate or inadequate response to a child's unique characteristics.

While it is difficult to "know what you do not know," a child care provider should develop strategies for reflection and self-assessment when concerned about a child and take appropriate steps for support.

- **Be open to learning.** While it is difficult to "know what you do not know," a child care provider should develop strategies for reflection and self-assessment when concerned about a child and take appropriate steps for support. The more a provider has to work with children who have disabilities or other special needs, the more sophisticated his (or her) questions will become.

- **Provide the modifications or adaptations recommended.** When working with specialists or families, a child care provider must be prepared to carry out their suggestions for successful inclusion. The provider must also inform others if more clarification or demonstration is needed to implement the strategy. In support of this, it is important to have a plan that enables a child care provider to monitor and evaluate the effectiveness of an intervention.

- **Know the applicable laws and regulations.** Child care directors and providers working from a family home should have specific training in the laws related to special education and early intervention, as well as in the federal Americans with Disabilities Act (ADA) and relevant California statutes on disabilities (see Appendix A, "Applicable Laws"). Knowledge of licensing regulations and of when and how to apply for waivers for serving children with disabilities (especially those with special health care needs) is also critical.

- **Be familiar with community resources.** Child care providers can find out which agencies in the community provide services and/or support to children and families and get to know the individuals from those agencies and develop relationships with them. Knowledge of resources that may benefit the family of a child with special needs can make a huge difference in the quality of support or the appropriateness of a referral that a child care provider is able to give a child.

- **Gather more information.** It may be appropriate to get specific training related to an individual child's disability or special need. It may also be desirable to take additional workshops and courses on inclusion; seek technical, on-site support; and/or participate in peer groups focused on inclusion.

Working with Specialists

Parents are a child care provider's first and most important resource. To obtain other specialist resources, a child care provider must have the parent's written consent. Or the parent must request the specialist to contact the provider.[13]

A child care provider may, of course, use other staff members to do problem-solving without specific parental consent, but everyone should be respectful and aware of confidentiality issues when doing this.

Individuals Available as Resources

Many different agencies provide services for young children with disabilities or special needs and their families: school districts, early intervention agencies, regional centers, public health agencies, family resource centers, therapy centers, and so on.

Specialists working with the child and family may come from a wide variety of backgrounds: special education, speech and language, early intervention, behavioral/mental health, nursing, social work, vision, occupational therapy, physical therapy, deaf and hard of hearing, assistive technology, and so on.

These specialists may be willing to provide staff development at the request of the child care program. (If the information shared by the specialists raises questions about a particular child, the family must be included in any discussion or visits.)

- If a child is already receiving services from an early intervention program, special education program at a public school, or therapists or other providers, a child care provider may ask the family for permission to communicate with the service providers. A family may also ask specialists to provide services or support to their child within the child care program itself.

- How to assist a child in participating more fully in a child care program is not always self-evident. Almost all child care providers—especially those who are expanding their inclusive efforts—need ideas for

A child care provider may use other staff members to do problem-solving without specific parental consent, but everyone should be respectful and aware of confidentiality issues when doing this.

communicating with children with special needs. They also want help in positive behavioral support techniques and generally welcome any other kind of support that a specialist can provide.

- Linking specialists with a child care program, in partnership with families, expands intervention efforts and helps to secure even greater positive outcomes for all children.

Specialists as Resources

Specialists act as consultants who support and provide resources to child care programs and family members. Specialists can:

- Share information specific to a child with special needs.
- Provide services to a child within the program or classroom.
- Exchange information on typical development.
- Give suggestions to be implemented into the daily routine.
- Observe the child and give feedback.
- Demonstrate techniques.
- Suggest resources, agencies, and services available in the community.
- Find answers to questions.
- Provide written information.
- Include the child care provider in the educational documents for the child and family (the IFSP for children under age three, or the IEP for children over age three).
- Specify in the IFSP or IEP a plan for direct consultation with the child care program by the specialist.

Coordination with Specialists and Families

The best way to coordinate child care efforts with those of specialists and families depends on the needs of the child, the family, and the care provider. Ideally, the family, provider, and specialist meet together to discuss the specialist's role in the child care program. Working together often leads to discovering the best way to share information and discuss how to best meet the needs of the child, the family, and the child care program. After the specialist's roles in this setting are articulated, along with any specific agreements on the part of the family or child care setting, it would be wise for the child care provider to record the agreements in writing. Once those are established, then everyone involved may also want to determine when the agreements will be reviewed. A sample agreement form is provided in Appendix C, "Agreement Form."

Working together often leads to discovering the best way to share information and discuss how to best meet the needs of the child, the family, and the child care program.

6

Examples of Inclusive Child Care Strategies

Inclusive child care takes place in many different ways, depending on the setting and the needs of the children in the program. This chapter offers several case studies that illustrate the unique strategies different programs have used to meet the needs of the children. Although a variety of strategies is used in each case to support the sense of belonging and inclusion of the children described, one primary strategy is highlighted for each (also see chapter 3, "Creating Inclusive Child Care Settings"). The studies are based on real children and programs, with names and identifying details changed to maintain confidentiality. These studies are designed to inspire and encourage child care providers who are working to develop inclusive settings.

1

STRATEGY 1

Environmental Support

Setting: Family Child Care
Child: Li
Age: Three years

BACKGROUND

Li is three years old and lives in a beach community. A quiet, sweet-natured little girl with a lot of determination, she was born prematurely and, as a result, has a significant visual impairment and mild delays in language and cognitive development, including difficulty in feeding herself. Li lives with her parents, Tran and Phuong, and is an only child. She has been attending the Jackson Family Child Care home since she was fourteen months old. Li's parents had previously used Tran's mother to care for their daughter, but when the grandmother developed health problems, they needed to find other care. Although nervous about using someone who was not a member of the family, they both needed to work. The family found the Jackson home through their early intervention provider, who had provided service at the Jackson home in the past.

Terry Jackson has 12 children enrolled in her center and employs two helpers, one in the morning and one in the afternoon. Terry had provided care for another child who had been born prematurely; however, that child had needs different from Li. Terry wondered how she would address Li's visual and developmental needs. The ideas from the early intervention specialist had been helpful in caring for the previous child, so she was optimistic about taking advantage of the same resource in providing effective care for Li.

SERVICES

Li received Early Start early intervention services specified in an IFSP until she was three years of age. Through this service, an early intervention specialist made visits to the Jackson family child care home alternate weeks, and a vision specialist made monthly visits. The early intervention team visited her at home on alternate weeks. The early interventionist and service coordinator worked with the family and provider in designing a transition plan since service providers change when a child reaches age three.

Li had made a transition to receiving services from the local school district through an IEP. Terry Jackson was able to attend the IEP meeting with the family, the early interventionist, the service coordinator, and representatives from the school district. After

Li received Early Start early intervention services specified in an IFSP until she was three years of age.

35

development of the IEP, the team discussed where the services would be provided. The family requested that Li remain at the Jackson home with support from the district, as the family had become quite comfortable with this arrangement. Before this instance, the school district had not provided services in a family child care home, but the personnel agreed on the arrangement.

STRATEGY

Because Li has a visual impairment, the environment was the primary area that needed modification. She could make some visual distinctions: she could see shapes six inches away and could distinguish between strongly contrasting colors. However, many environmental modifications were needed in order to support her inclusion. It was important that the modifications were made noticeable to Li. First, furniture was moved so that it defined the border between the family room and dining room, which was up one step, thus protecting Li from tripping on that step. Additionally, large removable stickers were placed on the sliding glass door that led outside, ensuring that Li would not walk into the glass. The toys that Li liked to play with were kept in the same place every day, and other children were encouraged to return them to the same shelf in order to assist Li in locating them independently. Containers of toys were a color that contrasted with the toys inside. This strategy also helped Li find what she was interested in.

Toys and materials themselves needed modification, as well. For example, Li liked to play with containers and take things in and out. Many containers were adapted so that the edges were more visible: a permanent marker or colored tape was applied to darken the edge. Li also needed clear contrast between her food and the plate or bowl she was using. So Terry planned which color of plates and bowls to use, depending on the food being served. Beyond her need for contrasting colors, Li preferred that her food did not have mixed textures (e.g., a casserole). As an accommodation, Terry worked with Tran and Phuong to develop ideas for menus. Terry also asked the specialist for resources on feeding children with special needs.

The toys that Li liked to play with were kept in the same place every day, and other children were encouraged to return them to the same shelf in order to assist Li in locating them independently.

In addition to her own learning, Terry made sure that both helpers had a chance to learn from the specialists, since Li's needs required the attention and involvement of everyone at the center. For example, an adult needed to keep a special eye on Li when the children were all playing. To help everyone in the learning process, Terry keeps a list on hand as questions arise.

One thing everyone learned was that the activities needed to be adjusted. Terry noticed that Li was hesitant to join the larger groups. Terry made a special point of keeping the groups small by having more than one interesting activity going on at a time. The specialists offered helpful ideas about ways to encourage Li to use her body when moving through the environment. An orientation-and-mobility teacher from the school district went so far as to create an obstacle course that Li especially enjoyed. As it turned out, all of the other children seemed to enjoy it as well.

Terry was able to participate in one of the IFSP meetings and was actively involved in planning for the transition-to-school services and the IEP for Li at age three. With the knowledge she had gained from the early intervention specialists and the developing relationship with the preschool specialists, Terry was sure that she could continue to provide a quality learning environment for Li.

SUPPORTING FACTORS

- The family had a strong relationship with the child care provider.
- The child care provider had a prior relationship with the specialist and was comfortable asking for help and ideas.
- The specialists were able to visit the environment where the child spent much of her time and offer ideas for modifications.
- All providers at the child care were involved in providing support and creating modifications for Li.
- The child care provider was able to play an active role in the planning meetings (IFSP and IEP) and in the discussion on transition.

As a result of the above factors, Li and her family received continuity in care and services and experienced a smooth transition between early intervention and special education.

An orientation-and-mobility teacher from the school district went so far as to create an obstacle course that Li especially enjoyed.

2

STRATEGY 2

Materials Adaptation

Setting: Military Child Care Center
Child: Danny
Age: Two and one-half years

BACKGROUND

Danny is two and one-half years old and lives on a military base. Talkative and social, Danny was born with spina bifida, a spinal defect that affects his ability to move his legs and control his bladder and bowels. He also has hydrocephalus (increased fluid around the brain), which has been treated with a shunt (a tube that allows fluid to drain and be absorbed into his body). He has been hospitalized several times for surgery on his shunt and feet, but not in the past eight months. Danny seems relatively healthy now. He wears leg braces to keep his legs straight and protected. He moves by rolling and scooting on his bottom. He talks quite well, mainly in phrases of two or three words. Although he seems to understand what is said to him, he does not have a long attention span. He lives with his mother, Crystal, who is in the Marine Corps. He began attending the child care center on the military base when he was twenty-two months old.

SERVICES

Danny receives early intervention services from a public school early intervention program. He is visited weekly by an early interventionist at the child care center and occasionally at home. He is also seen in his home by physical and occupational therapists from the early intervention program. The doctors on the base and at the clinic of the local children's hospital all closely follow his medical care.

STRATEGY

As Danny became more interested in playing with the toys and children in the center, the providers realized they needed help in making the materials accessible and usable for him. At the invitation of the staff at the center, the therapists and early interventionist made visits to observe Danny in the environment and then held a meeting with Crystal and the providers to share ideas.

As Danny became more interested in playing with the toys and children in the center, the providers realized they needed help in making the materials accessible and usable for him.

As a result of the suggestions, materials at the center were modified in several ways. Some toys and art supplies were placed on lower shelves to give Danny easier access. After careful observation of his interests, the providers moved toy cars from a tabletop to the floor. A table easel was placed on the floor so that Danny could sit and paint. Nonskid backing was added underneath the paint tray so that the paint did not tip as Danny scooted over to it. The sensory table was waist high to children who were standing. This table was used only when Danny had an adult available to hold him or get a chair for him. Since sensory toys were a high-interest activity for Danny, smaller tubs were filled with his favorite sensory toys and materials and made available on low shelves for him whenever he wanted. Because heavy toys were difficult for Danny to hold while scooting, lighter-weight toys and blocks were also provided. The toys enabled him to initiate play with other children and join in their play.

In addition, Danny was encouraged to ask his friends and teachers for help when he wanted something. The providers agreed to pay attention to his requests and interests when considering other materials to adapt. His IFSP team (consisting of the parent, specialist, and child care provider) also decided to explore some type of wheeled toy that Danny could use when he wanted to join the other children riding tricycles. After hearing all of these ideas, Crystal became interested in also getting a wheelchair for Danny.

SUPPORTING FACTORS

- The child's interests were observed and respected.
- Specialists were available to observe the child and give ideas.
- Materials were provided in a different form or were adapted to meet the child's needs.

The toys enabled him to initiate play with other children and join in their play.

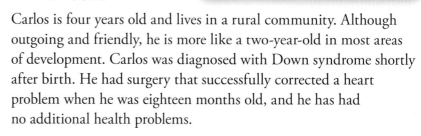

③

STRATEGY 3

Activity Simplification

Setting: Head Start Center
Child: Carlos
Age: Four years

BACKGROUND

Carlos is four years old and lives in a rural community. Although outgoing and friendly, he is more like a two-year-old in most areas of development. Carlos was diagnosed with Down syndrome shortly after birth. He had surgery that successfully corrected a heart problem when he was eighteen months old, and he has had no additional health problems.

Carlos lives with his mother, Maria, his two older sisters, and one older brother. His mother speaks primarily Spanish, and his siblings are bilingual. His fourteen-year-old sister often cares for him. Carlos was enrolled in the Head Start center at the beginning of the year. He attends four afternoons a week.

SERVICES

Carlos attends a special education class three mornings a week. He attended the class last year as well. His mother had her other children enrolled in Head Start and wanted Carlos to attend when he turned four. She has asked that his special education teachers work with the Head Start staff so that Carlos can receive bilingual speech therapy at the Head Start center with other children from his class.

STRATEGY

Carlos plays with toys like a child younger than four. He often put toys in his mouth and has trouble using his hands and fingers on small objects. His Head Start teachers are interested in learning how to modify materials so Carlos can play alongside his peers in the class. They also want to support his growth and development in playing with toys and his small-muscle movement. One of the Head Start teachers was able to visit Carlos' special education class and get ideas for suitable toys and activities. The Head Start disability specialist had previously supported many children with Down syndrome and had several ideas to contribute. Carlos' mother and his sister also helped by letting the team know what his favorite toys were at home.

The Head Start teachers are interested in learning how to modify materials so Carlos can play alongside his peers in the class.

40

The first and most important modification was to carefully examine all of the toys available in the classroom, looking for small parts that could be a danger if Carlos put them in his mouth. Any toys that were considered dangerous were used only under careful adult supervision. Second, toys that Carlos enjoyed were provided in larger form along with similar toys. Providers were initially worried that they would be forced to use "baby" toys to meet Carlos's needs, but they were pleasantly surprised at how easy it was to find age-appropriate materials. For example, in a tub that was filled with one-inch cube blocks, larger blocks were added, some with magnets or fabric hook-and-loop closures that allowed Carlos to successfully stack them. Cars, trucks, and airplanes with large wheels and removable people were brought in near other wheeled toys. Cardboard books (some in Spanish, others bilingual) were placed alongside the paperback books. Some books were taken apart and placed in photo albums, resulting in thicker pages that were easier for Carlos to turn.

In the arts and crafts materials area, three sets of special loop scissors were borrowed from special education personnel; these allowed Carlos to cut with minimum effort; the extra scissors also allowed his friends to try them as well. Larger markers and crayons were added to the supply. Duct tape was wrapped around the handles of sponge paintbrushes to make the handles larger. While helping Carlos work through activities, staff members gave Carlos only the materials he needed for one step at a time and helped him to think methodically through the directions for any activity. They often found that they only had to simply repeat directions given to the other children—but one at a time.

The teachers kept Carlos and all of these new strategies in mind when they thought of new materials and activities. As a result, he continued to gain skills while having fun playing with his friends. Carlos blossomed at Head Start, and his teachers from the special day class came to observe him. They were able to encourage his new skills in the special education classroom and learned some new things about Carlos.

SUPPORTING FACTORS

- The family was involved in planning for toys and materials.
- The internal resources available supported access to various toys.
- The Head Start staff and special day class staff were able to learn by observing Carlos in a different setting.

Some books were taken apart and placed in photo albums, resulting in thicker pages that were easier for Carlos to turn.

4

STRATEGY 4

Child Preferences

Setting: On-Campus, After-School Program
Child: Luke
Age: Eleven years

BACKGROUND

Luke is an eleven-year-old boy with cerebral palsy. He lives with his mother, Joy, and younger brother in an urban city. Luke has always received support in the regular class from the special education teacher. Luke has learning disabilities, and his mobility is affected by cerebral palsy. He is able to walk and run for short distances but loses his balance on occasion and gets tired when walking long distances. He and his brother attend an after-school child care program on the campus of their elementary school.[14]

SERVICES

Luke is in the fifth grade and receives services from the resource specialist, speech therapist, and adaptive physical education teacher at school. He has been attending the after-school program for two years. In the past, there has been little overlap between the specialists and the after-school program. At first, the after-school providers were uncomfortable with Luke's lack of balance, which resulted in his occasionally falling. Because the providers wanted to avoid an injury, they tried to restrict his outdoor activity by

Luke receives services from the resource specialist, speech therapist, and adaptive physical education teacher at school.

placing him with a group of younger children when the older group was outside or on field trips in the neighborhood. He did not like the indoor games offered, however, and started getting into trouble.

STRATEGY

After talking with his mother, the after-school providers decided to spend some time talking with Luke about what it was he wanted to do after school. They discovered that he wanted to play basketball and go on field trips with the oldest group. He also was good at computer games and wanted the program to have some for him to play.

In looking carefully at Luke's preferences, the providers clearly saw that he was asking to do activities different from what the after-school providers had been offering him. The first thing they did was obtain permission from Joy to talk with the adaptive physical education teacher at the school site and get some ideas for ways to handle the occasional falls and things to do if Luke were injured. Then, on field trip days, his mother brought in his bicycle so that he could go out with the group and keep up. Next, the program, which previously had a policy against computer games, obtained some games for a donated computer and made playing the computer games one of Luke's choices during the time he spent indoors. Luke now had an opportunity to demonstrate his skill at many of the games. As a result, he was also given leadership responsibilities for teaching and supervising the younger children as they played those games. To support continual efforts to adapt Luke's after-school setting, the family also requested that the IEP specifies regular consultations with the after-school program and reciprocal visits to gain information, ideas, and support.

In looking carefully at Luke's preferences, the providers clearly saw that he was asking to do activities different from what the after-school providers had been offering him.

SUPPORTING FACTORS

- Luke was able to participate in his program development by sharing his interests and ideas.
- The after-school child care provider was open to new ideas from the child, the family, and other adults working with Luke.
- Information was shared between the special education program and the child care program, with consultations planned for the future.

5

STRATEGY 5

Special Equipment

Setting: Family Child Care
Child: Jessie
Age: Eleven months

BACKGROUND

Jessie is eleven months old and lives in a suburb of a highly industrialized California city. Jessie was born prematurely and was hospitalized for the first ten weeks of her life. Now, at the age of eleven months, she has mild developmental delays and a chronic respiratory illness. Jessie lives with her parents, Dawn and Kirk. Finding appropriate child care was challenging for Dawn because Jessie requires daily medications by mouth and nebulizer treatments up to four times a day. Jessie's parents' work schedules consist of long commutes and four, 12-hour workdays. With assistance from a local child care resource and referral agency, Jessie's mom found a licensed family child care provider, Maya, who serves eight children near Jessie's home and can provide care during the extended hours needed by the family.

SERVICES

Jessie receives California Early Start early intervention services according to an individualized family services plan (IFSP) developed by the local regional center. Her medical condition is carefully monitored, and she has many appointments. The mother's work schedule allows her to have one weekday at home with Jessie for the medical and special service appointments Jessie needs. During naptime at the family child care provider's home, an IFSP meeting was held with the parents, the regional center service coordinator, a developmental specialist, and the child care provider. Together they developed a plan for early intervention and for coordinating services, along with a special care plan in case of emergencies. At this meeting, Maya expressed some concern about Jessie's medical conditions. She had previous experience caring for children with special needs, but none with these particular issues.

The mother's work schedule allows her to have one weekday at home with Jessie for the medical and special service appointments Jessie needs.

STRATEGY

After signing appropriate medical release forms and checking with licensing, Dawn trained Maya to administer Jessie's medications and nebulizer treatments. Maya also contacted the local lung association and Jessie's health-care provider for additional training and information on the use of inhaled medications. Dawn worked closely with the child care provider and her back-up assistants to ensure that someone who knew how to care for Jessie was on site at all times.

The developmental specialist from the Early Start program now visits Jessie at the child care provider's home once a week to provide ideas for promoting Jessie's developmental skills and addressing her health care needs. Maya is able to integrate some of these activities for promoting development into the regularly scheduled program. In this way, the activities become a part of the curriculum for all children's growth and development, and Maya feels confident in the care she is providing.

SUPPORTING FACTORS

- Services were coordinated among specialized service providers, the child care provider, and the family.
- The child care provider received specialized training prior to the child's enrollment in the program.
- Good communication between service providers and the family allowed services to be provided in a fashion appropriate to the group setting.

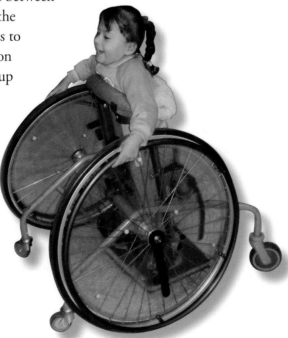

The developmental specialist from the Early Start program now visits Jessie at the child care provider's home once a week to provide ideas for promoting Jessie's developmental skills and addressing her health care needs.

STRATEGY 6A

Adult Support

Setting: Subsidized, Center-Based Child
    Care and Development Program
Children: Andrea, Jamal, and Tamika
Age: Three years, four years, and three
    and one-half years

BACKGROUND

City Child Care Center is a subsidized child care and development program. The program has 24 children in the three-year-olds' class, two teachers, an aide, and often a foster grandparent. All three providers have had some training or experience in serving children with special needs, of which there are three in the class. Each has very different needs; however, they all have in common a significant delay in speech and language.

Andrea is three years old and full of energy. She has a significant hearing loss and wears a hearing aid, although she often takes it off and gives it away to friends or buries it in the sandbox. Andrea smiles constantly and seeks interaction with children and adults. She can verbalize a few words and is sometimes frustrated in groups, probably because she cannot hear what is happening. She communicates best with facial expressions and gestures and is beginning to use a little sign language.

Jamal is four years old and has been at the center for two years. During that time, he was diagnosed as having autism. Because of this condition, Jamal loves predictability and routine. His favorite activity has been lining cars up or spinning their wheels. He is attached to one of the teachers, and, for that reason, he has remained with the three-year-olds' class. Jamal speaks in memorized sentences (dialogue from TV shows or stories); however, he does not consistently use words to communicate with others. He has only recently begun to pay attention to the other children and adults.

Tamika is three and one-half years old and likes to observe for a long time before joining in. She interacts best in smaller groups of children and is often happiest being rocked by the foster grand-

The program has 24 children in the three-year-olds' class, two teachers, an aide, and often a foster grandparent.

6A

46

mother. Tamika has mild cerebral palsy and speech delays. She has recently been introduced to sign language and seems to like using it.

SERVICES

Four mornings a week Andrea attends a program for children who are deaf and hard of hearing and receives special services in that setting. California Children's Services (CCS) covered expenses for Andrea's hearing aid (see Appendix B, "Resources," for more information on CCS). Jamal and Tamika attend a special education preschool class together three mornings a week. Jamal receives additional visits to his home two mornings a week. Tamika receives speech therapy once a week and also monthly physical and occupational therapy consultations with CCS. The City Child Care Center developed an interagency agreement with the school district that provides services to Jamal and Tamika. As a result of the agreement, the district provides staff members who train the providers, visit the City Child Care Center program monthly, and extend invitations to the providers to attend the IEP meetings (with parental permission).

STRATEGY

The teachers decided to take a sign language class so that they could better support Andrea's and Tamika's communication development. The supervisor was able to reimburse them for their class fees through a fund for professional development. The teachers, in turn, taught the hand signs to their aide and the foster grandparent during nap-time. When they began using sign language in the program, they encouraged all of the children to sign when they communicated with

The City Child Care Center developed an interagency agreement with the school district that provides services to Jamal and Tamika.

47

Andrea and Tamika. Additionally, the providers received training from Jamal's specialist on strategies to increase his participation, including using picture boards to help him predict his activities and to use in his efforts to communicate.

Interestingly enough, the sign language excited Jamal. Because he did not sleep during naptime, which had been a problem in the past, the teachers discovered that he loved watching them practice sign and would ask them to sign the alphabet and numbers over and over again. They readily responded to his requests and, as a result, found themselves—and Jamal—rapidly developing the skill. In the meantime, Andrea and Tamika (along with many of the other children) responded to the picture communication boards used for Jamal. The teachers made up picture cards for everything, using toy catalogs, photographs, and the picture symbols shared by the speech therapist.

The classroom became abuzz with communication. All the children dramatically increased their language and communication skills. Jamal began interacting with the other adults and children through sign language. Tamika used sign language and pictures at first, but toward the end of the year she began using words and sentences and voluntarily stopped relying so much on sign language. Andrea became much less frustrated in her efforts to communicate and more comfortable in using sign language. She, too, was using words in addition to the sign language by the end of the year. The supervisor decided to keep the entire class and the same providers together for the next school year in order to sustain the gains in the communication-rich environment.

SUPPORTING FACTORS

- The child care providers had specialized training in using sign language and picture communication.
- Structured interventions were designed for each of the children with special needs, and these interventions were then integrated into the regular class setting.
- Interagency agreements allowed providers to be given training and services to be administered in the child care environment.

The supervisor decided to keep the entire class and the same providers together for the next school year in order to sustain the gains in the communication-rich environment.

48

STRATEGY 6B

Adult Support

Setting: Private Community Preschool
Child: Thomas
Age: Five years

BACKGROUND

Thomas has lived with his Aunt Mabel since he was six months old and had only intermittent contact with his biological parents. Thomas is extremely active, and Mabel tries to keep up with him as much as possible. He is enrolled in the Oceanview Child Care Center, a full-day program located in a coastal resort community. Thomas is big for a five-year-old and has had numerous episodes of out-of-control behavior at child care and at home. These behaviors include acting out and hitting other children. Mealtime and circle time are particularly difficult for Thomas, as he always wanders during those scheduled periods when the children are expected to sit.

SERVICES

The providers wanted to make a referral to the local school district so that Thomas could be considered for special education services, but his aunt has refused to request an assessment. Mabel felt that Thomas's parents were not consistent in their discipline with him, and she was hoping that, by socializing with other children, he would learn appropriate behaviors. No one was injured or

Mealtime and circle time are particularly difficult for Thomas, as he always wanders during those scheduled periods when the children are expected to sit.

seriously hurt during any of Thomas's episodes, but he had been observed charging across the room with scissors in hand. The providers began to worry that, with this kind of unpredictable behavior, Thomas would eventually end up hurting either himself or another child.

The child care director met with Mabel to talk about Thomas's behavior and the effect it was having on him and other children. Mabel told the director that she was struggling with setting boundaries and felt that her disciplinary methods continually failed because she was too tired to enforce them after a long day at work. She noted that evenings were one of Thomas's best times, because he played in the swimming pool until he was tired and usually went to bed shortly thereafter.

STRATEGY

The director of the center developed a "behavior contract" with Mabel as a condition of Thomas's continued enrollment. This contract required her to attend an all-day parenting class offered on a Saturday by the local child care resource and referral agency. Child care was provided during this parenting class. She also referred Mabel to family counseling that was covered under her insurance plan. The director hoped that therapy would help Mabel better understand Thomas's behaviors and how to implement changes in her disciplinary practices. She also asked Mabel to visit the care center in order to observe the impact of Thomas's behavior on the child care setting. She hoped these activities would prompt Mabel to reconsider an assessment by the local special education agency in her area.

In addition, the child care center staff agreed to provide Mabel with a daily behavior log of Thomas's day, hour by hour. The center director also provided her with a pamphlet on managing difficult behavior. Mabel agreed to the conditions of the contract, and the center was able to continue to serve Thomas.

Family therapy ended up making a significant difference for Thomas and Mabel. Because of what Mabel learned in the process, she came to see clearly that Thomas did not know when he was behaving appropriately or inappropriately. Ultimately, three months after starting therapy and after an incident in which Thomas injured another child, Mabel consented to a school district assessment, which established Thomas' eligibility for special education services. The

The director of the center developed a "behavior contract" with Mabel as a condition of Thomas's continued enrollment.

therapist working with Mabel and Thomas consulted with the special education team and director and developed a plan for supporting Thomas in the community preschool setting.

Staff members had noticed that Thomas was particularly fond of Della, one of the teacher's assistants. Because she enjoyed him as well, she was assigned the task of giving him extra attention. An early childhood special educator trained Della to help Thomas recognize appropriate and inappropriate behavior.[15] In one particularly effective strategy, Della held a sign showing the green side when Thomas' behavior was appropriate and then showing the red side when his behavior was inappropriate. Other than changing the sign from green to red, she ignored his negative behavior, thus not letting him experience it as a way to get attention.

In addition, she learned many ways of acknowledging and reinforcing his appropriate behavior. Thomas quickly learned to keep his sign green, which marked for him a transitional step toward developing self-control.

Mabel also learned similar activities for use at home. In both home and care settings, Thomas's improved self-control allowed the stop sign system to be gradually reduced, as his episodes of unmanageable behavior decreased. By the time he was scheduled to make the transition into kindergarten, he was ready. His child care providers expected him to manage successfully without extra support services.

SUPPORTING FACTORS

- Thomas's child care providers accepted the guardian's (Mabel's) timelines for getting services while being clear about keeping Thomas and his peers safe.
- A parenting class, with child care, was available in the community and taught Mabel how to manage Thomas's difficult behavior at home.
- The communication between home and school occurred respectfully, regularly, and with agreed-upon outcomes.
- The adult selected to support Thomas was someone he liked and with whom he already had a relationship.[16]
- When additional services were received, the child care providers worked with the school district to coordinate and implement a plan and then support the changes in behavior.

In one particularly effective strategy, Della held a sign showing the green side when Thomas' behavior was appropriate and then showing the red side when his behavior was inappropriate.

STRATEGY 7

Peer Support

Setting: Community College Lab School
Child: Sofia
Age: Four years

BACKGROUND

Sofia is very shy, has good walking and movement skills, loves playing with dolls, and has been receiving special services since her premature birth.

Sofia is four years old and lives with her parents, Eduardo and Jamira, in a suburb of a large California city. Sofia's parents are originally from Brazil and are taking classes at the community college. Sofia is very shy, has good walking and movement skills, loves playing with dolls, and has been receiving special services since her premature birth. She has delays in language, cognitive, and small motor development. She has been at the campus lab school in the morning program for over one year.

SERVICES

Sofia currently attends a language/speech therapy group two afternoons a week at the local elementary school. An early childhood special education teacher visits the campus lab school at least once a month. The providers at the school were invited by her parents to attend the last IEP meeting and were able to provide much information about Sofia's interactions at school. Lately they have been concerned that Sofia was keeping to herself and playing almost exclusively with dolls in a way that was more typical of a younger child.

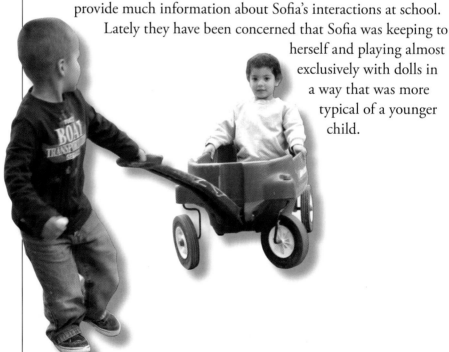

STRATEGY

As a way of helping Sofia interact with other children, another girl was sought out who also enjoyed dolls. Robyn was asked to be Sofia's buddy. All of the children were paired with buddies in order to make the doll activity part of the larger group. The specialist from the school taught Robyn some ways of getting Sofia's attention and encouraging Sofia to play with the dolls as Robyn did. The head teacher learned the techniques, as well. The providers also made the dramatic center larger so that several buddies could play there at the same time; and the student interns were coached in ways to encourage interaction through the comments they made observing the children at play. In addition, different kinds of dolls were provided in the home center that potentially encouraged more developmentally advanced play: dolls in various kinds of dress and with different hair, babies and older dolls, and boy dolls and girl dolls. Gradually, different props were added (beds, high chairs, food) to the area, and other buddies began playing more actively with Sofia and Robyn.

Having a buddy helped Sofia move into other areas of the classroom. With a doll under her arm, she became very comfortable following Robyn into the block area, the book area, and other places beyond the home center. Providers would gently offer her something from the other play areas to encourage her to expand her play beyond the dolls; and they would comment on what the other children were doing, especially Sofia's partner, Robyn. Sofia began to leave the doll in the home center when moving around the classroom and started to interact with other children.

SUPPORTING FACTORS

- Another child in the program shared Sofia's interests.
- The specialist was able to train the peer and the providers in ways to encourage interaction.
- The providers used their knowledge of child development to expand and encourage more mature play skills.

Providers would gently offer her something from the other play areas to encourage her to expand her play beyond the dolls; and they would comment on what the other children were doing, especially Sofia's partner, Robyn.

STRATEGY 8

Invisible Support

Setting: Private, After-School Program
Child: Erica
Age: Eight years

BACKGROUND

Erica, eight years old, lives with her parents, Jeff and Debbie, and is the older of two girls. The family lives in a city in the Central Valley. Erica is active and loves to skate, but she has some challenges in reading. Erica recently started complaining that she did not like going to her after-school program and did not have any friends there. She was also complaining of not having friends at school. Jeff met with the after-school staff members to discuss what was happening in school and to see what ideas the staff members had. The staff members expressed concern about Erica's behavior and thought that her strong personality and desire to have activities done her way were interfering with her ability to make friends in the program.

SERVICES

Erica was receiving resource services to help her with reading. She was already being monitored for some behavior challenges in the classroom, specifically those related to her interactions in small groups. She was working on impulse control in the classroom, and her parents were satisfied with the progress she was making at school. But they were concerned about the latest reports from the after-school staff.

STRATEGY

Jeff was able to share with the staff members in the after-school program some of the strategies that the classroom teacher was using to support Erica's interactions with other children. Because Erica tended to go to whichever group was the loudest and most active, it often meant that an activity was already in progress and the group was formed. Moving from this observation, the staff members (borrowing an idea from Erica's classroom) made clothespins with the children's names on them. A card was made for each activity. Lines on the card indicate the maximum number of clothespins that can be clipped to it. The card lets the children know how many

The staff members expressed concern about Erica's behavior and thought that her strong personality and desire to have activities done her way were interfering with her ability to make friends in the program.

of them could participate in an activity at one time. Then Erica was given support to select an activity and stay with it until there was a room for her clothespin in a different activity. The clothespins were also used as a way of determining whose turn if only one child at a time could participate. The child with the clothespin on the first line went first, and the rest of the children took turns from there. This visual reminder helped Erica wait for her turn. When she interrupted, the other children simply pointed to the card.

The staff members found that other children appreciated the smaller groups and the new, visual reminder of taking turns. In addition, Erica began to interact well with a couple of other children, and the staff members began to encourage them to take part in small-group activities together. Erica started getting along with the other children and eventually was invited to several birthday parties. By the end of the year, she had two good friends. Additionally, a staff member from the after-school program attended Erica's next IEP meeting at the father's invitation with the intention of increasing the coordination and collaboration between the settings.

SUPPORTING FACTORS

- The family shared strategies from the school classroom.
- The after-school staff members were able to implement changes that supported many children.
- Paying attention to the children's interest and interaction helped to nurture friendships.
- A relationship between staff of the after-school program and staff of the school program was initiated.

Erica began to interact well with a couple of other children, and the staff members began to encourage them to take part in small-group activities together.

Appendixes

Appendix A
Applicable Laws

State and federal laws provide protection for people with disabilities.

The Americans with Disabilities Act

The Americans with Disabilities Act (ADA) is federal legislation that was passed in 1990. The ADA guarantees civil rights protection to people with disabilities in areas such as employment, transportation, public accommodations, and child care. Both child care centers and family child care homes must comply with the ADA, whether they are privately or publicly funded. The only exemptions allowed are for religious organizations operating child care programs. The ADA provides protection to a child or adult who meets any of the following criteria:

- Has a physical or mental impairment that substantially limits one of the "major life activities"
- Has a record of such an impairment
- Is regarded as having an impairment
- Is associated with an individual with a disability

The ADA mandates that "reasonable accommodations" be made in child care for children with disabilities. In most cases, the accommodations needed are quite simple and inexpensive to implement. For instance, a child with diabetes may need a snack at a different time or more frequently than other children; or a child who has difficulty making the transition to different activities may need a little extra time and support to do so. The ADA also makes it clear that the child care program may not charge families of children with disabilities higher fees than other families pay.

The ADA also mandates that architectural barriers to entering or using facilities be removed when this is "readily achievable." This phrase means that those necessary changes that do not place "an undue burden" on a provider need to be made ("an undue burden" is defined as a "significant difficulty or expense"). Examples of readily achievable designs could involve rearranging furniture for a child with visual impairments, installing a handrail in the bathroom for a child who uses a walker, changing door hinges, or other similarly minor accommodations. By making these relatively simple accommodations, a child care provider is complying with the ADA.

There are instances in which accommodation involve more significant changes. Fortunately, there are tax credits and other resources that can help offset the cost of these more extensive alterations to the child care setting (see the ADA Web site in Appendix B, "Resources" for more information).

The ADA also acknowledges that there may be a situation in which a child may not be admitted to the child care program if the child would pose a direct threat to others, if the modification would fundamentally alter the program itself, or if the accommodation needed would be an undue hardship to the program. These exceptions are considered on an individual basis, and the law expects child care providers to work hard to include children with disabilities as often as possible.

California's Unruh Civil Rights Act

Every state has the option of enacting provisions that provide more protection than the federal Americans with Disabilities Act (ADA). California has the Unruh Civil Rights Act, *California Civil Code* Section 51, which is much more expansive than the ADA and offers even broader protection for children with special needs. Unlike the ADA, it provides protection from discrimination by *all* business establishments in California, including housing and public accommodations. California's law may apply even to religious entities, although there have not been published legal opinions where that has been tested.

IDEA and Child Care

Both Part C and Part B of the IDEA strongly emphasize a collaborative relationship between parents and teachers/providers in the development of services. Parents may invite child care providers to participate in the development and implementation of IFSPs and IEPs. Participation in this process is an excellent opportunity for child care providers to share knowledge about the child in their care and to assist in coordinating services for that child. Families can also request that consultation or direct services from early intervention and special education programs be provided in the child care setting.

The Individuals with Disabilities Education Act

The Individuals with Disabilities Education Act is federal legislation mandating special education for all eligible children.[17] The Individuals with Disabilities Education Improvement Act of 2004 (IDEA 2004) is the most recent reauthorization of the statute. The IDEA guarantees children with disabilities a free, appropriate public education; an education in the least restrictive environment; related services; and fair assessment in the delivery of those special education services to children, from birth to age twenty-two. The law has four parts: Part A covers the general purpose of the law and definitions; Part B addresses the requirements for the education of all children with disabilities from age three through age twenty-one; Part C covers the specific requirements for services to infants and toddlers (children from birth to thirty-six months) with disabilities and their families; and Part D authorizes national activities to improve special education services (research, personnel development, technical assistance, and state improvement grants).

The IDEA makes it possible for states and localities to receive federal funds to assist in the education of infants, toddlers, preschoolers, children, and youth with disabilities. Essentially, in order to remain eligible for federal funds under the law, states must ensure the following:

- All children and youth with disabilities, regardless of the severity of their disability, will receive a free, appropriate public education (FAPE) at public expense.
- The education of children and youth with disabilities will be based on a complete and individual evaluation and assessment of the specific, unique needs of each student.
- An individualized education program (IEP) or an individualized family services plan (IFSP) will be drawn up for every child or youth found eligible for early intervention or special education, stating precisely what types of early intervention services or what kinds of special education and related services or each infant, toddler, preschooler, child, or youth will receive.
- To the maximum extent appropriate, all children and youth with disabilities will be educated in the regular education environment. Children and youth receiving special education have the right to receive the related services they need to benefit from special education instruction.
- Parents have the right to participate in every decision related to the identification, evaluation, and placement of their child or youth with a disability.
- Parents must give consent for any initial evaluation, assessment, or placement; they must be notified of any change in placement that may occur; they must be included, along with teachers, in conferences and meetings held to draw up IEPs; and they must approve these IEPs before they go into effect for the first time.
- The right of parents to challenge and appeal any decision related to the identification, evaluation, and placement—or any issue concerning the provision of FAPE—of their child is fully protected by clearly spelled-out due process procedures.
- Parents have the right to have information kept confidential. No one may see a child's records unless the parents give written permission. Once a child has an IFSP or IEP, parental consent is needed for anyone to discuss the child with others. (The exception to this is school personnel who have legitimate educational interests.)

Part C in California: Early Start

As mentioned above, Part C of IDEA addresses services for infants and toddlers. California's state law that implements this component of the IDEA is the California Early Intervention Services Act, the state's early intervention program for infants and toddlers from birth through thirty-six months. This state act is guided by both federal and state laws. The Department of Developmental Services is the lead agency for Early Start and collaborates with the California Department of Education, Department of Social Services, and several other state agencies to provide services to infants and toddlers who have a developmental disability or who are at risk of developmental disabilities.

Children and families eligible for the Early Start program qualify for early intervention services. Regional centers share primary responsibility with local educational agencies (school districts and county offices of education) for coordinating and providing these services at the local level.[18] They may include specialized instruction, speech and language services, physical and/or occupational therapy, and transportation.

Infants and toddlers may be identified and referred to regional centers or local educational agencies (LEAs) through primary referral sources in their communities, including hospitals, health-care providers, child care providers, LEAs, social service programs, or the child's family. Each infant or toddler referred to Early Start receives an evaluation to determine eligibility and, if eligible, an assessment to determine service needs.[19] The individualized family services plan (IFSP) is the legal document that describes the services the child is receiving. IFSPs are reviewed at least every six months, and child care providers are welcome to participate in these meetings, as long as they have the permission of parents. The participation of child care providers in these meetings may be especially important if the child is receiving any early intervention services at the child care program's site.

Federal and state laws emphasize that early intervention services should be provided in "natural environments" whenever possible. Natural environments are those places where the child and family would be if the child did not have a disability, such as the home or a child care program. Therefore, a parent may approach service providers about providing intervention at their child care program itself. Welcoming a therapist or an early interventionist into a child care program is a positive way for a child care provider to promote inclusion and enrich the program as a whole.

Early Start also provides funding for 55 resource centers throughout the state that provide parent-to-parent support to families with infants and toddlers with special needs. These Family Resource Centers/Networks (FRC/Ns) are staffed primarily by parents and provide support in a nonclinical, family-centered environment. Specifically, FRC/Ns provide referral information and outreach to underserved populations, they support child-find activities and family/professional collaborative activities, and they assist families with transition.[20]

Services for Children Three to Twenty-Two Years of Age

As briefly discussed, Part B of the IDEA applies to children three to twenty-two years of age who qualify for special education services. The California Department of Education oversees the implementation of Part B services in the state, as do departments of education in other states across the country.

There have been several revisions to the IDEA over the years, and the latest strengthens provisions concerning "least restrictive environments." This term means that, to whatever extent possible, children should be in the same classes as their typically developing peers. For children ages three to five, this means that specialized services are ideally provided in settings such as the home, child care center, or family child care home. For this age group, services are provided through the local school district, county office of education, or special education local planning area (SELPA).

Special education provides specific early education programs for children between the ages of three and five who have disabilities. These programs include individual and group services in a variety of typical, age-appropriate environments for young children, such as regular child care programs, the home, and special education preschool programs. Services are based upon ongoing consultations with the family, include related support services for the child and family, and are provided in the least restrictive environment.

See "Information About Laws" in Appendix B, "Resources," for more information.

Appendix B

Resources

The following resources were compiled in April 2009, and the information was accurate as of that time. Because of frequent changes of information, a section on the California Map to Inclusive Child Care Web page has current links to all resources mentioned below. Please visit the Web site, and click on the menu item labeled "Inclusion Works!" to link to the resources.

California Map to Inclusive Child Care

Web site: http://www.cainclusivechildcare.org/camap/

The new Web site for the California Map to Inclusive Child Care Project is operated by the Center for Child and Family Studies at WestEd and funded by the California Department of Education's Child Development Division. This comprehensive Web site devoted to the issue of inclusion and disabilities includes the links listed below.

California State Agencies

California Department of Education

The California Department of Education (CDE) oversees the state's diverse and dynamic public school system that is responsible for the education of more than seven million children and young adults in more than 9,000 schools. The CDE and the State Superintendent of Public Instruction are responsible for enforcing education law and regulations and for continuing to reform and improve public elementary school programs, secondary school programs, adult education, some preschool programs, and child care programs. The CDE's mission is to provide leadership, assistance, oversight, and resources so that every Californian has access to an education that meets world-class standards. The CDE is committed to working in partnership with local schools to improve student achievement.

Child Development Division
1430 N Street, Suite 3410
Sacramento, CA 95814
Telephone: 916-322-6233
Fax: 916-323-6853
Web site: http://www.cde.ca.gov/sp/cd/

In support of the California Department of Education's mission, the Child Development Division (CDD) provides leadership and support to all individuals and organizations concerned with children and families by promoting high-quality child development programs. The division works to educate the general public about developmentally appropriate practices for infants, toddlers, preschoolers, and school-age children in a variety of safe and healthy child care and child development environments. The goal is for children and families to be balanced, lifelong learners. The CDD Web site provides descriptions about child development programs administered by the Department, important information for child development contractors, legal and regulatory requirements, and resources for child development contractors, families, and the child care community.

Special Education Division
1430 N Street, Suite 2401
Sacramento, CA 95814
Telephone: 916-445-4613
Fax: 916-327-3516
Web site: http://www.cde.ca.gov/sp/se/

The home page for the California Department of Education, Special Education Division, links to current information about services and programs provided by the Department. The division's mission is to serve the unique needs of individuals with disabilities (from birth to twenty-two years) so that each person will meet or exceed high standards of achievement in academic and nonacademic skills. This achievement will be represented by the ability of each person, in natural and formal settings, to demonstrate successful personal, vocational, and social interaction, including transition to the workplace and independent living. The division believes that each individual with a disability should be embraced and the rights of all to equity and access are guaranteed.

Before & After School Program
1430 N Street, Suite 6408
Sacramento, CA 95814
Telephone: 916-319-0923
Web site: http://www.cde.ca.gov/ls/ba/

The home page for the California Department of Education, Before & After School Program includes links to programmatic and fiscal resources to build, implement, and sustain quality before and after school programs, including school-age care and other out-of-school opportunities for children and youth.

California Department of Developmental Services
P.O. Box 944202
Sacramento, CA 94244-2020
Web site: http://ww.dds.ca.gov

The California Department of Developmental Services (DDS) is the agency through which the state of California provides services and varieties of support to children and adults with developmental disabilities. These disabilities include mental retardation, cerebral palsy, epilepsy, and autism and its related conditions. DDS is California's lead agency for services for children birth to three years of age, as defined under Part C of the Individuals with Disabilities Education Act (IDEA '04). There are several Web links for agencies and services related to Early Start: California Early Start: http://www.dds.ca.gov/earlystart/home.cfm

Family Resource Center/Network: http://www.dds.ca.gov/earlystart/familyresources.cfm

Regional Centers: http://www.dds.ca.gov/rc/home.cfm

California Department of Health Care Services, Children's Medical Services Branch, California Children's Services

714/744 P Street
P.O. Box 942732
Sacramento, CA 94234-7320
Telephone: 916-445-4171
Web site: http://www.dhs.ca.gov/

California Children's Services (CCS)
Web site: www.dhcs.ca.gov/services/ccs/pages/default.aspx

The Children's Medical Services Branch provides a comprehensive system of health care for children through preventive screening, diagnoses, treatment, rehabilitation, and follow-up services. It is a full-scope management system for California Children's Services and the Genetically Handicapped Persons Program.

California Department of Mental Health

Programs for Children and Youth
1600 Ninth Street, Room 151
Sacramento, CA 95814
Telephone: 916-654-3890 or 800-896-4042
Fax: 916-654-3198
E-mail: dmh.dmh@dmh.ca.gov
Web site: http://www.dmh.ca.gov/services_and_programs/children_and_youth/default.asp

The California Department of Mental Health administers several programs for children and youth. The programs' services are directly provided at the local level by counties and their contract providers. To obtain local mental health services, contact your local county mental health agency.

California Department of Social Services
744 P Street
Sacramento, CA 95814
Telephone: 916-651-8848
Web site: http://www.cdss.ca.gov

Community Care Licensing Division
Web site: http://www.ccld.ca.gov

The mission of the California Department of Social Services is to serve, aid, and protect needy and vulnerable children and adults in ways that strengthen and preserve families, encourage personal responsibility, and foster independence.

First 5 California (California Children and Families Commission)
2389 Gateway Oaks Drive, Suite 260
Sacramento, CA 95833
Telephone: 916-263-1050
Fax: 916-263-1060
Web site: http://www.ccfc.ca.gov

The California Children and Families Act of 1998 was also known as Proposition 10 and is now First 5 California. Many of its activities include children with special needs, and its Web site has links to local county CCF commissions and much more.

California Training & Technical Assistance Organizations

The organizations in this section provide technical assistance and/or training that may be useful to child care providers, preschool staff, after-school staff, specialists, or families who are developing or supporting an inclusive setting for children. State organizations are listed here. Information about local training and technical assistance may be available through your local child care resource and referral agency or your local Early Start family resource center (see below).

**Beginning Together: Caring for Infants and Toddlers with Disabilities
or Other Special Needs in Inclusive Settings**
Telephone: 760-682-0200
Fax: 760-471-3862
E-mail: beginningtogether@wested.org

Web site: http://www.cainclusivechildcare.org/bt/

Beginning Together was created in collaboration with the California Department of Education, Child Development Division (CDD) and WestEd, Center for Child and Family Studies as an inclusion support to the Program for Infant/Toddler Caregivers.

The purpose of Beginning Together is to ensure that strategies to include children with special needs are incorporated in the training of caregivers and appropriate inclusive practices are promoted.

California Preschool Instructional Network (CPIN)
Telephone: 800-770-6339
E-mail: cpin@wested.org
Web site: http://www.cpin.us/

California Preschool Instructional Network (CPIN) provides professional development and technical assistance to preschool teachers and administrators to ensure that preschool children are ready for school. The CPIN is divided into the 11 regions designated by the California County Superintendents Educational Services Association (CCSESA). There is a regional lead, a special education lead, and an English learner lead stationed in each of the 11 regions throughout the state of California.

CalSTAT (California Services for Technical Assistance and Training)
Fax: 707-586-2735
E-mail: info@calstat.org
Web site: http://www.calstat.org

CalSTAT (California Services for Technical Assistance and Training) is a special project of the California Department of Education, Special Education Division, located at Napa County Office of Education. It is funded through the Special Education Division and the California State Personnel Development Grant (SPDG). The SPDG, a federal grant, supports and develops partnerships with schools and families by providing training, technical assistance, and resources to both special education and general education.

Center for Prevention & Early Intervention (CPEI)
Telephone: 800-869-4337
Fax: 916-492-4002
E-mail: cpei@wested.org
Web site: http://www.wested.org/cs/cpei/print/docs/230

WestEd's Center for Prevention and Early Intervention in Sacramento provides statewide high-quality training, technical assistance, resource development, and support to state agencies and community programs that administer or provide prevention and early intervention services. The state agencies have included the California Departments of Education, Developmental Services, Health Services, Social Services, Mental Health, and Alcohol and Drug Programs.

Desired Results access Project
Telephone: 707-227-5963
E-mail: info@draccess.org
Web site: http://www.draccess.org

Desired Results access Project assists the California Department of Education, Special Education Division (SED), in implementing the Desired Results Developmental Profile (DRDP) assessment system to measure the progress of California's preschool-age children who have individualized education programs. The Desired Results access Project Web site offers information and resources to assist special educators, administrators, and families in participating in the Desired Results assessment system.

Kids Included Together (KIT) National Training Center on Inclusion
Telephone: 858-225-5680
Fax: 619-758-0949
E-mail: info@kitonline.org
Web site: http://www.kitonline.org/ntci/home.html

KIT National Training Center on Inclusion (NTCI) was established to support its overall mission through training, technical assistance, and resources of the highest quality for staff in out-of-school-time programs at all levels of experience and interest. Its National Training Center on Inclusion uses a combination of the latest technology coupled with live presentations by dynamic and experienced trainers and practitioners to support providers in welcoming children with disabilities.

Least Restrictive Environment (LRE) Resources Project
Telephone: 916-492-4013
E-mail: dmeinde@wested.org
Web site: http://www.wested.org/cs/cpei/view/pj/204

The Least Restrictive Environment (LRE) Resources Project, operated by WestEd for the California Department of Education, develops resources for use by school districts and sites to improve services for all students. To achieve this goal, the project is establishing a network of leadership sites and consultants that focuses on teacher training, mentoring, facilitation, technical assistance, and specialized materials.

Special Education Early Childhood Administrators Project (SEECAP)
Telephone: 760-761-5526
E-mail: kfinn@sdcoe.net
Web site: http://www.sdcoe.k12.ca.us/student/eeps/seecap/?loc=home

Special Education Early Childhood Administrators Project (SEECAP) is a project of the California Department of Education, Special Education Division. It is coordinated by the San Diego County Office of Education, Early Education Services and Programs

Unit. This professional development project was instituted in support of research indicating that there is a direct relationship between quality early intervention programs and the knowledge, skills, and attitudes of the administrators who run those programs.

Supporting Early Education Delivery Systems Project (SEEDS)
Telephone: 916-228-2379
Fax: 916-228-2311
E-mail: rryan@scoe.net
Web site: http://www.scoe.net/SEEDS

The SEEDS Project assists the California Department of Education in providing technical assistance to early childhood special education programs. With the direction of the CDE, SEEDS has established a network of consultants and visitation sites to assist local educational agencies in providing quality services.

California Parent Organizations

Family Resource Center Network of California (FRCNCA)
E-mail: info@frcnca.org
Web site: http://www.frcnca.org

The FRCNCA is a coalition of California's 47 Early Start family resource centers. Staffed by families of children with special needs, the family resource centers offer parent-to-parent support and help parents, families, and children locate and use needed services. They offer support services and resources in many languages: newsletters, resource libraries, Web sites, parent-to-parent groups, sibling support groups, warmlines, and information and referral for parents and professionals.

Other California Parent Organizations
Web site: http://www.cde.ca.gov/sp/se/qa/caprntorg.asp

The site identifies California agencies providing resources for families of children with disabilities including Parent Training and Information Centers, California Community Parent Resource Centers, and Family Empowerment Centers.

Professional Organizations

American Speech-Language-Hearing Association (ASHA)
10801 Rockville Pike
Rockville, MD 20852
Telephone: (Voice or TTY) 800-638-8255
E-mail: actioncenter@asha.org
Web site: http://www.asha.org

The American Speech-Language-Hearing Association (ASHA) is the professional, scientific, and credentialing association for more than 103,000 audiologists, speech-language pathologists, and speech, language, and hearing scientists. ASHA's mission is to ensure that all people with speech, language, and hearing disorders have access to quality services to help them communicate more effectively.

The Division for Early Childhood (DEC)
634 Eddy
Missoula, MT 59812-6696
Telephone: 406-243-5898
Fax: 406-243-4730
E-mail: dec@selway.umt.edu
Web site: http://www.dec-sped.org

The Division for Early Childhood (DEC) is an organization designed for individuals who work with—or on behalf of—children with special needs, birth through age eight, and their families. DEC, a subdivision of the Council for Exceptional Children (CEC), is dedicated to promoting policies and practices that support families and enhance the optimal development of children. Children with special needs include those who have disabilities or developmental delays, are gifted/talented, or are at risk of future developmental problems.

Infant Development Association of California (IDA)
P.O. Box 189550
Sacramento, CA 95818-9550
Telephone: 916-453-8801
Fax: 916-453-0627
E-mail: mail@idaofcal.org
Web site: http://www.idaofcal.org

The Infant Development Association of California (IDA) is a multidisciplinary organization of parents and professionals committed to optimal developmental and positive social and emotional outcomes for infants, birth to three, with a broad range of special needs and their families. IDA advocates improved, effective prevention and early intervention services while providing information, education, and training to parents, professionals, decision makers, and others.

National Association for the Education of Young Children (NAEYC)
1313 L Street NW, Suite 500
Washington, DC 20005
Telephone: 202-232-8777 or 800-424-2460
Fax: 202-328-1846
E-mail: naeyc@naeyc.org
Web site: http://www.naeyc.org

The National Association for the Education of Young Children (NAEYC) is the nation's largest organization of early childhood professionals and others dedicated to improving the quality of early childhood education programs for children birth through age eight. NAEYC's primary goals are to improve professional practice and working conditions in early childhood education and to build public understanding and support for high-quality early childhood programs.

Zero to Three
2000 M Street NW, Suite 200
Washington, DC 20036
Telephone: 800-899-4301
Web site: http://www.zerotothree.org

Zero to Three is a national, nonprofit organization dedicated solely to advancing the healthy development of babies and young children. Zero to Three disseminates key developmental information, trains providers, promotes model approaches and standards of practice, and works to increase public awareness about the significance of the first three years of life.

National Disability and Inclusion Resources

Center for Inclusive Child Care (CICC)
Toll-free: 866-948-2222
Telephone: 719-687-0735
Fax: 719-687-8114
Web site: http://www.inclusivechildcare.org

The mission of the Center for Inclusive Child Care is to create, promote, and support pathways to successful inclusive care for all children. The program is a comprehensive resource network for inclusive early childhood, school-age programs, and providers. The CICC provides leadership, administrative support, training, and consultation to early care and education providers, school-age care providers, parents, and professionals in the field.

Disability Is Natural
Toll-free: 866-948-2222
Telephone: 719-687-0735
Fax: 719-687-8114
Web site: http://www.disabilityisnatural.com

This Web site created by Kathie Snow includes her widely used article on "people-first language" and other resources to support inclusion. She challenges outdated ways of thinking and helps parents, people with disabilities, and professionals acquire new perceptions and attitudes—the first rung on the ladder of change.

The Family Village
Waisman Center
University of Wisconsin-Madison
E-mail: familyvillage@waisman.wisc.edu
Web site: http://www.familyvillage.wisc.edu

The Family Village is a global community that integrates information, resources, and communication opportunities on the Internet for persons with mental retardation and other disabilities, for their families, and for those that provide services and support. The Web site includes information on specific diagnoses, communication connections, adaptive products and technology, adaptive recreational activities, education, worship, health issues, disability-related media and literature, and more.

Fathers Network
Telephone: 425-653-4286
Web site: http://www.fathersnetwork.org

The Fathers Network is a nonprofit organization that serves as an advocate for men and believes they are crucially important in the lives of their families and children. The network provides supports and resources to fathers and families of children with developmental disabilities and chronic illness and to the professionals who serve them.

National Child Care Information and Technical Assistance Center (NCCIC)
Telephone: 800-616-2242
Fax: 800-716-2242
TTY: 800-516-2242
E-mail: info@nccic.org
Web site: http://www.nccic.org

The National Child Care Information and Technical Assistance Center (NCCIC), a project of the Child Care Bureau, Administration for Children and Families (ACF), U.S. Department of Health and Human Services, is a national resource that links information and people in order to complement, enhance, and promote child care delivery systems. The organization works to ensure that all children and families have access to the highest quality comprehensive services.

National Early Childhood Technical Assistance Center
Telephone: 919-962-2001
TDD: 919-843-3269
Fax: 919-966-7463
E-mail: nectac@unc.edu
Web site: http://www.nectac.org

The National Early Childhood Technical Assistance Center supports the implementation of the early childhood provisions of the Individuals with Disabilities Education Act (IDEA). The center's mission is to strengthen service systems to ensure that children with disabilities (birth through five) and their families receive and benefit from high-quality, culturally appropriate, and family-centered supports and services.

National Information Center for Children and Youth with Disabilities (NICHCY)
Telephone (Voice/TTY): 800-695-0285
Fax: 202-884-8441
E-mail: nichcy@aed.org
Web site: http://www.nichcy.org

The NICHCY is the national information and referral center that provides information on disabilities and disability-related issues for families, educators, and other professionals. One special focus is children and youth (birth to age twenty-two). Many publications are available in Spanish.

National Professional Development Center on Inclusion (NPDCI)
E-mail: community@mail.fpg.unc.edu
Web site: http://community.fpg.unc.edu/npdci

The National Professional Development Center on Inclusion (NPDCI) is working with states to ensure that early childhood teachers are prepared to educate and care for young children with disabilities in settings with their typically developing peers.

Information About Laws

Americans with Disabilities Act (ADA)
Web site: http://www.usdoj.gov/crt/ada/adahom1.htm
Child care page: http://www.ada.gov/childq&a.htm

Disability Rights Section of ADA mailing address:

U.S. Department of Justice
Civil Rights Division
Disability Rights Section-NYAV
950 Pennsylvania Avenue, NW
Washington, DC 20530
ADA Information Line: 800-514-0301

Commonly Asked Questions About Child Care Centers and the Americans with Disabilities Act is a 13-page publication that explains how the requirements of the ADA apply to child care centers. It also describes some of the Department of Justice's ongoing enforcement efforts in the child care area, as well as a resource list on sources of information on the ADA. This document is available at the Web site listed above and can also be requested by fax. To order a publication by fax, call the ADA Information Line and follow the directions for placing a fax order. When prompted, enter the document number: 3209.

Child Care Law Center
221 Pine Street, Third Floor
San Francisco, CA 94104
Telephone: 415-394-7144
Fax: 415-394-7140
E-mail: info@childcarelaw.org
Web site: http://www.childcarelaw.org

The Child Care Law Center (CCLC) is a national, nonprofit legal services organization founded in 1978. The CCLC's primary objective is to use legal tools to foster the development of high-quality, affordable child care for every child, every parent, and every community. The CCLC works to expand child care options, particularly for low-income families, and to ensure that children are safe and nurtured in care outside the home. It is the only organization in the country that focuses exclusively on the complex legal issues surrounding the establishment and provision of child care.

Disability Rights California (California's protection and advocacy system)
Telephone: 800.776.5746 (voice)
Telephone: 800.719.5798 (TTY)
 E-mail: info@disabilityrightsca.org
Web site: http://www.disabilityrightsca.org/

Disability Rights California is a nonprofit disability rights organization working since 1978 to advance human and legal rights of Californians with disabilities. It strives to create a barrier-free, inclusive society that values diversity and each individual. Services are available throughout the state and assist tens of thousands of people with disabilities each year. More than 200 staff and board members have a wide array of legal and advocacy expertise. They have developed innovative programs for Californians with developmental, psychiatric, sensory, and physical disabilities. They collaborate on the state and federal levels with other advocacy groups throughout the U.S.

Disability Rights Education & Defense Fund
2212 Sixth Street
Berkeley, CA 94710
Telephone: 800-348-4232 (v/tty)
Telephone: 510.644.2555 (v/tty)
Fax: 510-841-8645
E-mail info@dredf.org
Web site: http://www.dredf.org/

The Disability Rights Education and Defense Fund, founded in 1979, is a leading national civil rights law and policy center directed by individuals with disabilities and parents who have children with disabilities.

Individuals with Disabilities Education Act (IDEA '04)
IDEA Partnership
Web site: http://www.ideapartnership.org

This site is part of a federal project to support the implementation of the Individuals with Disabilities Education Act (IDEA '04). The site answers questions about the IDEA and makes available the full text of the law and its regulations.

Appendix C
Agreement Form

An agreement form is used when services are coordinated among specialists, families, and child care providers. Although the IFSP or IEP lists specific outcomes for the child (and family), an agreement form is especially useful for listing those other questions that arise when a specialist is providing services in child care programs:

- Who will contact the specialist when the child is not at the child care center on the day of an expected visit?
- How will information be shared among the specialists, families, and child care providers (copies of visit notes, a journal or notebook that records events and agreements, phone contacts, etc.)?
- How will the services of the specialist be delivered in the child care program?
- How will equipment for a child to use in the child care program be shared or acquired?

Child's name _____

Meeting date: _____ Review date: _____

Family agrees to: _____

Signature: _____

Specialist agrees to: _____

Signature: _____

Child care provider agrees to: _____

Signature: _____

Appendix D
California Children Enrolled in Special Education

Special Education Category	Birth to Age 14	Birth to Age 6	Age 6 to Age 14
Specific Learning Disability	37.13%	5.93%	40.40%
Speech and Language Impairment	33.23%	58.31%	31.54%
Mental Retardation	5.18%	6.12%	4.90%
Other Health Impairment	7.18%	5.24%	7.30%
Autism	8.85%	14.66%	8.08%
Orthopedic Impairment	2.17%	3.48%	1.94%
Emotional Disturbance	2.70%	0.11%	2.79%
Hard of Hearing	1.40%	2.63%	1.17%
Multiple Disability	0.69%	1.23%	0.59%
Visual Impairment	0.65%	1.06%	0.57%
Deaf	0.58%	1.03%	0.48%
Traumatic Brain Injury	0.21%	0.14%	0.20%
Deaf-Blindness	0.03%	0.06%	0.02%

Source: Special Education Division, California Department of Education, December 2008

Endnotes

1. N. Kunc, "The Need to Belong," 25–39.
2. California Department of Education, *Early Warning Signs*.
3. Carnegie Corporation of New York, *Starting Points*.
4. R. Peth-Pierce, *National Institute of Child Health and Human Development Study of Early Child Care*.
5. Child Care Aware, *Choosing Quality Child Care for a Child with Special Needs*.
6. S. Bredekamp, ed., *Developmentally Appropriate Practice in Early Childhood Programs*, 8–9.
7. J. R. Lally and others, *Caring for Infants and Toddlers in Groups: Developmental Appropriate Practice* (Washington, DC: Zero to Three, 1995).
8. National Child Research Center brochure.
9. J. Lieber and others, "Key Influences on the Initiation and Implementation of Inclusive Preschool Programs," *Exceptional Children* 67(1).
10. P. L. Mangione, "Beginning Together and the Program for Infant/Toddler Caregivers."
11. S. R. Sandall and others, "Talking to Practitioners."
12. P. L. Mangione, "Beginning Together and the Program for Infant/Toddler Caregivers."
13. This section is adapted from a handout originally developed in 1998 by Linda Brault titled "Accessing Consultative Resources: A Guide for Child Care Providers."
14. Parts of this case study are inspired from a story in the video *Just a Kid Like Me,* which is no longer available for distribution.
15. Ideas for this behavior management system are similar to those found in H. M. Walker, "First Step to Success," as referenced in *Practical Ideas for Addressing Challenging Behaviors*.
16. This concept is more completely described in *Project Relationship: Creating and Sustaining a Nurturing Community*, a manual and video available through WestEd Center for Prevention & Early Intervention; telephone 800-869-4337.
17. National Dissemination Center for Children with Disabilities, *News Digest*.
18. California Head Start State Collaboration Office, *Bridges* 10, No. 2 (Summer 2005), 39–46.
19. Ibid., 4.
20. Ibid., 5–6.
21. These data were obtained from the California Department of Education DataQuest Web site at http://data1.cde.ca.gov/dataquest/.

Glossary

Like many professionals, early intervention and special education specialists have their own vocabulary. This glossary of common special education terms, compiled from a variety of sources, is included to help care providers when speaking with specialists. (The contents of this glossary do not necessarily represent definitions endorsed by the California Department of Education.)

ADA: Americans with Disabilities Act (see Appendix A, "Applicable Laws").

Assessment: A process using observation, testing, review of information, and analysis of a child's strengths and areas of need to plan appropriately for services and supports.

At-risk: A term used with children who have, or could have, delays or challenges in their development that may affect their later learning.

Child care program: Any setting that provides care for children by paid personnel, which includes child care and development centers, family child care homes, in-home child care, after-school programs, Head Start centers, and the like. The personnel at these settings may be referred to as providers, teachers, caregivers, or staff.

Child find: A service directed by each state's department of education for identifying and diagnosing unserved children with special needs.

Children who are typically developing: Children who display development and behavior in the expected range for their age.

Children with disabilities or other special need: Children with a specific diagnosis, as well as children who do not have a diagnosis but whose behavior, development, and/or health affect their family's ability to maintain child care services. The disability or special need may be as mild as a slight speech delay or as complex as a mixed diagnosis of motor challenges, vision impairment, and cognitive delays. Generally, this definition includes those children who are between birth and twenty-two years of age and who are protected by the Americans with Disabilities Act.

Children with exceptional needs (a child development definition aligned with special education: California *Education Code* Section 8208[l]): Children who have been determined to be eligible for special education and related services by an individualized education program team according to the special education requirements contained in Part 30 (commencing with Section 56000) and who meet the eligibility criteria described in Section 56026 (see below) and Sections 56333 to 56338, inclusive, and Sections 3030 and 3031 of Title 5 of the *California Code of Regulations*. These children have an active individualized education program and are receiving appropriate special education and services, unless they are under three years of age and permissive special education programs are available. These children may be developmentally disabled, hard-of-hearing, deaf, speech-impaired, visually handicapped, seriously emotionally disturbed, orthopedically impaired, other health impaired, deaf-blind, or multihandicapped; or children with specific learning disabilities that require the special attention of adults in a child care setting.

Children with special needs (a child development definition: California *Education Code* Section 8208[m]): The term includes infants and toddlers under the age of three years; limited-English-speaking-proficient children; children with exceptional needs; limited-English-proficient handicapped children; and children at risk of neglect, abuse, or exploitation.

Due process: An action that protects a person's rights. In special education, this applies to action taken to protect the educational rights of students with special needs in areas of identification, evaluation, service delivery, or placement.

Early intervention (applies to children eligible for California's Early Start Program): Services for infants and toddlers (birth through thirty-six months of age) with disabilities and their families. Early intervention services may include, but not be limited to, the following: special instruction for the child, service coordination, family counseling and/or training, social work services, health services, medical services, audiology services, speech therapy, occupational therapy, and physical therapy. Children are eligible for early intervention services if they exhibit developmental delays or have a diagnosed physical or mental condition that has a high probability of resulting in developmental delays in cognition, social/emotional behavior, adaptive behavior, communication, or physical development. Early intervention services are funded under Part C of the Individuals with Disabilities Education Act (IDEA '04).

Eligible: The child meets certain requirements to qualify for services.

Evaluation: A formal way of collecting information about a child's learning needs, strengths, and interests. An evaluation is part of the process of determining whether a child is eligible for early intervention or special education programs and services.

Family member (or parent): The person with primary responsibility for raising the child. Examples include mother, father, foster parent, and grandparent.

Family Resource Centers/Networks—Early Start (FRC/N): Agencies funded by the California Department of Developmental Services to provide parent-to-parent support, education, training, and other services to families with children from birth to thirty-six months of age who have, or are at risk of, a developmental disability.

IDEA: Individuals with Disabilities Education Act (see Appendix A, "Applicable Laws").

Identification: The process of locating and identifying children needing special services.

Inclusion: The full and active participation of children with disabilities or other special needs in community activities, services, and programs designed for typically developing children, including child care. If support, accommodations, or modifications are needed to ensure full, active participation, they are provided appropriately. The participation results in an authentic sense of belonging for the child and family.

Individualized education program (IEP): A written plan for each child, from three to twenty-two years of age, who receives special education services. The IEP includes the following: statements of the present level of the child's functioning, annual goals, specific educational services needed, dates of service, a description of the recommended degree of participation in regular education programs, and procedures for evaluating the child's progress. The IEP must be signed by the child's parents (or legal guardians) and the educational personnel working with the child, including the general education teacher.

Individualized family services plan (IFSP): A written plan for each infant and toddler, from birth to three years of age in most states, who receives early intervention services. The plan outlines service and supports provided to the child and family. Services are family-focused and provided in the natural environment. The IFSP must contain a description of the child's level of development, strengths and needs, family concerns, priorities and resources, expected major outcomes, services needed, date of the next IFSP, and the starting date for services on the present IFSP.

Individualized program plan (IPP): A written plan for each child over three years of age who is receiving regional center services under the California Lanterman Act requirements.

Informed consent: A parent- or guardian-signed written consent that is required before any information about a child can be shared with, or released to, other agencies. Before they sign, parents/guardians must review all relevant information. All informed consent forms must be written in the parent's first or primary language.

Lead agency: The agency (office) within a state or territory that is in charge of overseeing and coordinating early intervention programs and services under the IDEA.

Least restrictive environment (LRE): Required by the IDEA, LRE applies to children between three and twenty-two years of age who are receiving special education services in settings and through activities where children who are typically developing may be found (e.g., regular class placement and child care settings). The IDEA states that children with special needs are to be educated with their nondisabled peers to the maximum extent appropriate. The law also states that removing a child from general education settings may occur only after it is determined that the severity or nature of the disability prevents the child from receiving effective education in the general education class. Amendments to the IDEA have strengthened the original law's commitment to the least restrictive environment.

Local educational agency (LEA): The school district or county office of education that is responsible for providing special education services to students with disabilities.

Natural environments: Those home and community settings that are most "natural" to the child. Most often they are places where a child's typically developing peers can also be found. Early intervention services are provided to children from birth to three years of age in the natural environment to the maximum extent appropriate, including home and community settings in which the infant or toddler without disabilities participates.

Parent: Any person living with a child who has responsibility for the care and welfare of the child. (See also *Family member*.)

Referral: A formal request to test a child to determine if he or she is in need of early intervention or special education services.

Regional centers: In California, a private, nonprofit organization responsible for providing services to persons with developmental disabilities from birth through adulthood through contract with the state Department of Developmental Services (DDS). DDS is the lead agency for early intervention services in California.

SELPA (Special Education Local Planning Agency): In California, the agency responsible for special education services within a geographic area.

SDC (special day class): A term used in public education to refer to a special education classroom for children who receive the majority of their instruction from the classroom teacher in that classroom.

Transition: A change from one environment or service delivery model to another (e.g., leaving early intervention services and entering preschool).

Bibliography

Abbott, C. F., and S. Gold. "Conferring with Parents When You're Concerned That Their Child Needs Special Services," *Young Children* 46(4): 10–14.

"Agencies Serving Young Children with Disabilities and Child Care Referral Agencies," *Bridges* 10(2): 39–46.

Bricker, D. "The Challenge of Inclusion" *Journal of Early Intervention* 19(3): 179–94.

Choosing Quality Child Care for a Child with Special Needs. Washington, DC: Child Care Aware/National Association of Child Care Resource and Referral Agencies and Easter Seals [n.d.] (brochure).

Developmentally Appropriate Practice in Early Childhood Programs. Edited by S. Bredekamp and C. Copple. Washington, DC: National Association for the Education of Young Children, 1997.

Early Childhood Inclusion: Focus on Change. Edited by M. J. Guralnick. Baltimore, MD: Paul H. Brookes, 2001.

Early Warning Signs. Sacramento: California Department of Education [n.d.] (brochure). (Now titled *Reasons for Concern.* Available in five languages free of charge. Telephone 800-995-4099.)

"The Education of Children and Youth with Special Needs: What Do the Laws Say," *NICHCY News Digest* 15 (1996).

"Finding Daycare for Robert," *Bridges* 4(1): 2–35.

Handbook on Developing and Implementing Early Childhood Special Education Programs and Services. Sacramento: California Department of Education, Special Education Division, 2001.

"Inclusive Child Care: Quality Child Care for All Children," *Child Care Bulletin* Issue 21.

Kunc, N. "The Need to Belong: Restructuring Maslow's Hierarchy of Needs," in *Restructuring for Caring and Effective Education: Administrative Guide to Creating Heterogeneous Schools.* Edited by R. A. Villa; J. S. Thousand; W. Stainback; and S. Stainback. Baltimore, MD: Paul H Brookes, 1992, pp. 25–39.

Lally, J. R., and others. *Caring for Infants and Toddlers in Groups: Developmentally Appropriate Practice.* Washington, DC: Zero to Three, 1995.

Lieber, J., and others. "Key Influences on the Initiation and Implementation of Inclusive Preschool Programs," *Exceptional Children* 67(1): 83–98.

Lynch, E. W.; M. Ballard-Rosa; and C. Cavallero. *Belonging, Not Just Being There: Inclusion for Infants, Toddlers, and Preschoolers with Disabilities.* San Diego: San Diego State University, Department of Special Education, 1996.

Mangione, P. L. "Beginning Together and the Program for Infant/Toddler Caregivers: A Partnership." Presentation given at the Beginning Together Institute, San Diego, California, October 2003.

McDonnell, A. P.; K. Brownell; and M. Wolery. "Teacher's Views Concerning Individualized Intervention and Support Roles within Developmentally Appropriate Preschools," *Journal of Early Intervention* 24(1): 67–83.

Odom, S. L., and others. "On the Forms of Inclusion: Organizational Context and Individualized Service Models," *Journal of Early Intervention* 22(3): 185–99.

Patten, P., and O. B. Ricks. "Child Care Quality: An Overview for Parents," *ERIC Digest*, EDO-PS-00-14 (2000).

Peth-Pierce, R. *The National Institute of Child Health and Human Development (NICHD) Study of Early Child Care*. 1998. http://www.nichd.nih.gov/publications/pubs early_child_care.htm (accessed October 22, 2001).

Room at the Table: Meeting Children's Special Needs at Mealtime. Sacramento: California Department of Education, California Child Nutrition and Food Distribution Division, 1998 (video and manual).

Sandall, S. R., and others. "Talking to Practitioners: Focus Group Report on Curriculum Modifications in Inclusive Preschool Classrooms," unpublished manuscript, 2001.

07-020 PR070079-0 05-09 10M

OSP 09 114571